LECTURES IN AMERICA

LECTURES
IN AMERICA

By

F. R. Leavis
and Q. D. Leavis

1969

Chatto & Windus

LONDON

Published by
Chatto & Windus Ltd
40 William IV Street
London W.C.2

*

Clarke, Irwin & Co. Ltd
Toronto

SBN 7011 1455 X

Printed in Great Britain by
R & R Clark Ltd
Edinburgh

CONTENTS

v

ACKNOWLEDGEMENTS

The quotations from *Collected Poems* by W. B. Yeats appear by permission of Mr M. B. Yeats and Macmillan & Co. Ltd., London, and The Macmillan Company, New York; and the quotations from *Collected Poems 1909–1962* by T. S. Eliot appear by permission of Faber & Faber Ltd., London, and Harcourt, Brace and World Inc., New York. © 1936 by Harcourt, Brace and World Inc. and © 1963, 1964 by T. S. Eliot.

PREFATORY NOTE

The lectures were given on our visit to the United States in October 1966.

The essay on *Wuthering Heights* is of course too long to have been delivered as it stands. The note that precedes it explains in what way it represents different lectures given at Cornell University and Adams House, Harvard University.

Two of my own lectures were given at both universities as they stand here. The third, which also has not been published before, I gave at an improvised meeting to an audience at Adams House. I had delivered it in the first place at the Queen's University, Belfast.

The whole visit was made possible by the generosity of Cornell University and of Adams House, which sponsored our visit to Harvard University. Our warmest thanks are due also for the hospitality we enjoyed at both places of learning, and especially to Professor Max Black, Director of the Society for the Humanities at Cornell University, and Professor R. A. Brower, Master of Adams House.

F. R. Leavis

I

Luddites?
or There is Only One Culture

LUDDITES?
OR THERE IS ONLY ONE CULTURE

I AM used to being misrepresented, but not resigned to it. Everyone who has committed himself in relation to the themes I discussed in my Richmond lecture, *Two Cultures?—The Significance of C. P. Snow*, and taken a line at all like that taken by me there, knows how gross and inconsequent is the misrepresentation that follows, and how impossible it is to get the case one has put attended to. Instead, something quite different is, explicitly and implicitly, associated with one's name and made the target for a routine play of contemptuous and dismissing reference. Of course, this kind of response represents a large element of willed refusal to see and understand—the will not recognizing itself for the thing it is by reason of a flank-rubbing consensus that is its sanction. But this element of refusal is an essential characteristic of the situation that the persuader has to deal with, and therefore, if one thinks the issues are of moment—and I do—one is not resigned.

You see, I am confessing to a touch of embarrassment: I don't want to seem to be attributing any of that unintelligent—or anti-intelligence—set of the will to the present audience as a general characterizing trait, but, in presenting as clearly as I can in positive terms and in a positive spirit (which is what I want to do) my view of the issues raised by the talk about the 'two cultures', I am bound to refer to the misrepresentations and misunderstandings that ought not by now to need answering but seem all the same to be the staple enlightenment about these issues so far as the publicity-practitioners, the formers of public opinion, are concerned.

And that, I must emphasize, is not merely at the lowest level. Mr Richard Wolheim, for example, who is a sociologist, I believe, remarked in *Partisan Review*, with an air of convicting me of insidious and significant evasion, that I had not in my Richmond lecture made clear whether I was *for* a high material standard of living or *against* it. My point of course had been this: that it won't do to make a rising material standard of living the self-sufficient aim on the confident assumption that we needn't admit any other kind of consideration, any more adequate recognition of human nature and human need, into the incitement and direction of our thinking and our effort: technological and material advance and fair distribution—it's enough, it's the only true responsibility, to concentrate on them; that's the attitude I confront.

Again, to take a very representative example of the habit of those who address the British intelligentsia, a writer in the *Spectator*, Sarah Gainham, who had earlier joined in the indignant outcry orchestrated in that journal against my 'attack' on Snow (which it had, at its own request, printed), ends a subsequent review of a German author with this:

> She was used to well-being, yet it is materialism for the mass of people to get used to well-being. This is a familiar resentment and envy, often seen in Britain, that working people should be going to Florence and Majorca, and buying Beethoven long-playing records. This ought not to be dressed up as moral indignation.

Of course it oughtn't, as far as it exists. And possibly the writer could back her 'familiar' by adducing instances known to her. But to suggest that such resentment and envy are representative, so that she can reasonably dismiss in this way all questioning uneasiness about the human consequences of the technological revolution and the affluent society—is that to promote clear vision and intelligent thought? The unrealism, the disturbing emotional intention, or perversity, betrays itself clearly enough in those 'Beethoven long-playing records'. I myself, after an unaffluent and very much 'engaged' academic life, am not familiar with Majorca or Florence, but in those once very quiet places very much nearer Cambridge to which my wife and I used to take our children the working-class people now everywhere to be met with in profusion carry transistors round with them almost invariably. The music that comes from these, like that one hears in greater volume in the neighbourhood of the Bingo establishments (of which the smallest coast-hamlet has at least one—Bingo being the most pathetic of vacuum-fillers) doesn't at all suggest aspirations towards Beethoven. If working-class people did, characteristically, or in significant numbers, show a bent that way, who would be found deploring it?—except, of course, Kingsley Amis and his admirers (and there you *have* a significant cultural phenomenon that Miss Gainham would do well to ponder). But as for the actual working-class people who *can* be regarded as characteristic, it's not anything in the nature of moral indignation one feels towards *them*, but shame, concern and apprehension at the way our civilization has let them down—left them to enjoy a 'high standard of living' in a vacuum of disinheritance. The concern, I imagine, is what all decent people capable of sympathetic perception must feel; the apprehension is for the future of humanity.

I shall hardly be accused of paradox here. It isn't very long since the *New Statesman*—*the New Statesman*, on whose Board of Directors it was natural for Snow to be, came out with a front-page article headed 'The Menace of Leisure'. That is an irony indeed—a richly charged one. I recall a passage of D. H. Lawrence's criticism which is especially useful to those faced with enforcing the point that Lawrence was no more given to Morrisian archaizing—garden-suburb handicraftiness—than to the Carlylean gospel of Work. The passage occurs in the 'Study of Thomas Hardy' which deserves more attention than it gets, and is to be found on page 425 of *Phoenix*:

> But why so much: why repeat so often the mechanical movement? Let me not have so much of this work to do, let me not be consumed so overmuch in my own self-preservation, let me not be imprisoned in this proven, finite existence all my days.
>
> This has been the cry of humanity since the world began. This is the glamour of kings, the glamour of men who had the opportunity to be . . .
>
> Wherefore I do honour to the machine and to its inventors.

An irony! Lawrence in 1915 does honour to the machine because it gives us leisure—leisure for living (and 'living', he adds, 'is not simply not dying'), and now, for the *New Statesman*, leisure is a menace.

But my immediate point regards the way in which any writer who is known as taking a less simple view of the development and human significance of industrial civilization than Lord Snow (or Lord Robbins) is dubbed 'Luddite', after the machine-breakers, and dismissed— the implication, or contention, being that literature tends in general to be the enemy of enlightenment in this matter. The term has come significantly into favour these last two or three years. Thus Lawrence is a Luddite. And not so long ago I read in the *Sunday Times* (or the other one of those British Sunday papers which have magazine sections in which culture gets a show) a book-notice in which the reviewer, discussing a work on the Victorian city, reeled off a list of names of distinguished Victorian writers as those of notorious Luddites in their attitude towards the new kind of urban development.

Well, though I think it serves no intelligent purpose to dub Carlyle and Ruskin 'Luddites', I could pass that with a shrug. And if Morris is dubbed 'Luddite', it doesn't move me to fierce indignation. But Arnold and Dickens! I will confine my necessarily brief commentary to Dickens, the great creative writer, for it is the dismissal of him that is most significant—I mean most revealing of the nature of the *parti pris* we have to do with in the general dismissal by the Neo-Wellsians of the thought and witness and the profoundly relevant creative energy represented by literature.

Dickens was a great novelist, and, as such, an incomparable social historian. It is the great novelists above all who give us our social history; compared with what is done in *their* work—their creative work—the histories of the professional social historian seem empty and unenlightening. Dickens himself lived intensely, experienced intensely at first hand a wide range of the life of his time, and was peculiarly well qualified to make the most of his opportunities of observing. His power of evoking contemporary reality so that it lives for us today wasn't a mere matter of vividness in rendering the surface; it went with the insight and intelligence of genius. The vitality of his art was understanding. In fact, as I have gone on reading him I have come to realize that his genius is in

7

certain essential ways akin to Lawrence's. He saw how
the diverse interplaying currents of life flowed strongly
and gathered force here, dwindled there from importance
to relative unimportance, settled there into something
oppressively stagnant, reasserted themselves elsewhere as
strong new promise. The forty years of his writing life
were years of portentous change, and, in the way only a
great creative writer, sensitive to the full actuality of
contemporary life, could, he registers changing England
in the succession of his books with wonderful vividness.

Except in so far as Coketown in *Hard Times* constitutes
an exception, Dickens doesn't deal with the industrial
city. The urban world of modern civilization for him is
London. And it is true that he presents it as a squalid,
gloomy and oppressive immensity, blighting and sinister
to the life it swarms with. But to make this justify our
classing Dickens as a Luddite is an odd—significantly
odd—proceeding. How much less than no excuse there
is for it can be brought out by recalling that in *Dombey
and Son*, Dickens's first great novel—one the organiz-
ing theme of which entails a critical presentment of
the contemporary civilization, the time being that of the
triumphant arrival of the railway age, he symbolizes the
human purpose and energy that must be looked to for an
escape from the squalor, misery and confusion by the
railway. There is that expedition in Chapter VI—Polly
Toodle, Paul's nurse, with Paul and Florence and Susan
Nipper—to Staggs's Gardens. On their way there they
pass through the scene of the great earthquake that has
rent Camden Town, where the new railway is being
driven through to Euston terminus. The evocation of
the scene is a magnificent and characteristic triumph of the
Dickensian genius. As I have noted in writing about the

book, we are reminded of those drawings, paintings and engravings in which the artists of that time record their sense of the Titanism and romantic sublimity of the works of man. It is not merely by the titanic audacity, but by the human promise above all, that Dickens is so profoundly impressed. He concludes:

> In short, the yet unfinished and unopened Railroad was in Progress, and from the very core of all this dire disorder trailed smoothly away upon its mighty course of civilization and improvement.

Dickens, the Luddite!—the note of this climactic sentence is not a casual inspiration, alien to the force and feeling of *Dombey and Son*. We have a dramatic presence, unmistakably essential to the book, and central here, in Toodle's answer to Dombey's questioning when Polly Toodle, his wife (the natural motherly woman, and as such herself essential to Dickens's creative theme), is being interviewed as the prospective wet-nurse who shall save little Paul's life: what has Toodle's work been?—

> Mostly underground, Sir, till I got married. I came to the level then. I'm agoing on one of these here railroads, when they comes into full play.'

The prosperity and happiness of the Toodle family are associated with the coming into full play of the railways, and seen as a representative accompaniment.

By way of insisting that this characteristic of *Dombey and Son* is characteristic of Dickens, I will just point to Daniel Doyce, the inventor, and his place in the scheme of values of *Little Dorrit*, that very great novel which, of all Dickens's larger works, is the most highly organized, everything in it being significant in relation to the whole —and the whole constituting something like an inquest into civilization in contemporary England. Doyce, genius of beneficent invention, and, in the face of the Circumlocution Office and the patronizing bourgeois (Meagles), invincibly sane, persistent and matter-of-fact, pairs with Cavalletto, the little Italian who puzzles the inhabitants of Bleeding Heart Yard by his simple ability to live and enjoy the sun: neither a major actor, they are major presences for the dramatic and poetic process of valuation implicit in Dickens's art because of what they so potently are and represent.

What I have been trying to bring out for clear recognition is the element of deep-seated refusal to perceive that betrays itself in such characteristic instances as I have adduced. We have it not only in the dead set at eliminating literature and what it represents from all serious relevance to the issues, but in the attitude towards *any* suggestion that the issues are essentially more complex than Snow's Rede lecture would make them, and fraught with other kinds of menace to humanity than he is able to recognize. There is that business of 'the old wheelwright's shop'— the play made with that phrase, thrown out with a knowing 'ha-ha' in the voice and manner, by a well-known Cambridge figure of the BBC world. The ironist is what Snow calls a 'literary intellectual', and the blind set of the will he relies on and means to confirm is that which had a representative illustration when a bright lady journalist in the *Spectator* quite wantonly dragged my name in as that (everyone knew) of the man to apply to if you wanted a wistful lament for the Old Style Pub (now vanished, I gather—for actually I know nothing about these things). The sole factual basis that could be alleged for these insinuations is the use to which, thirty years ago and more, Denys Thompson and myself in *Culture and*

Environment, a book for schools, put George Sturt's *The Wheelright's Shop*.

The use to which we put Sturt had nothing William-Morrisian in it; neither of us, I may say, went in for folk-dancing—or pubs. The attention we aimed at promoting was to the present, and our emphasis was on the need to understand the nature of the accelerating and inevitable change that was transforming our civilization. The wheelwright's business, we pointed out, or noted how Sturt pointed out, didn't merely provide him with a satisfying craft that entailed the use of a diversity of skills; it contained a full human meaning in itself—it kept a human significance always present, and this was a climate in which the craftsman lived and worked: lived *as* he worked. Its materials were for the most part locally grown, and the wheelwright quite commonly had noted as a tree *in situ* the timber that came to the shop—which is a representative aspect of the general truth. The customers too were local, and he knew them, themselves and their settings, as meeting their particular requirements he had to, individually—he, the wheelwright of the neighbour-hood. He saw the products of his craft in use, serving their functions in the life and purpose of a community that really *was* a community, a human microcosm, and couldn't help feeling itself one.

We didn't recall this organic kind of relation of work to life in any nostalgic spirit, as something to be restored, or to take a melancholy pleasure in lamenting; but by way of emphasizing that it was *gone*, with the organic community it belonged to, not to be restored in any foreseeable future. We were calling attention to an es-sential change in human conditions that is entailed by the accelerating technological revolution, and to the nature of the attendant human problem. And our sense that the problem was not likely to get all the attention it should be seen as demanding has been redundantly justified.

It is plain that the kind of relation between work and living documented in *The Wheelwright's Shop*, or anything like it, can't by any serious mind be proposed as an ideal aim in *our* world; that the only bearing it has on the possibilities we have to consider is that to recognize the nature of the change is to recognize the nature of the challenge, the problem that Snow ignores, a frightening characteristic that it has being to escape notice for what it is.

Mr Toodle of *Dombey and Son*, as stoker and aspiring engine-driver, had a job out of which he got much satisfaction, besides that of being able to support his family. He had there, we know, an advantage over the mass of industrial workers, and we have no difficulty in understanding how Dickens could present him as invested with a cheering significance for the human future. But the future we now see for the Toodles is automation, and the future seen as automation is what makes the *New Statesman* talk of the 'menace of leisure'. The development by which, for industrial workers, real living tends to be something thought of as saved for the leisure part of life is soon to be consummated. The meaninglessness, or human emptiness, of work will be sufferable because the working part of life will be comparatively short and the leisure part preponderant.

That this upshot of technological progress needs to be thought of as facing us with a problem is, as I've noted, receiving some kind of recognition: 'the menace of leisure', 'education for leisure', and so on—phrases of that kind give us the nature of the recognition. And my point is that such recognition is no real recognition of the problem that faces humanity. Certainly that problem is not being recognized for what it really is when discussion proceeds in terms of the need to educate for positive and more satisfying uses of his leisure the worker whose routine work, requiring or permitting no creative effort on his part, and no large active interest—little more, in fact, than automatisms—leaves him incapable of any but the passive and the crude.

We are *all* involved—and in the most intimate, inward and essential way; and not merely by reason of congested roads, the smell of fish and chips, the ubiquity of transistors and that kind of inconvenience, which is what, in England, discussion pertaining to the ethos of the *New Statesman* tends, however democratically (of course), to suggest. A general impoverishment of life—that is the threat that, ironically, accompanies the technological advance and the rising standard of living; and we are all involved.

Snow gives us a pregnant demonstration, very pertinent to the explaining of what I mean, when, as himself representative of his Two Cultures, he posits, to be set over against what he calls the 'scientific culture', a 'literary culture' that he represents by the literary intellectual of the *New Statesman* milieu, or the modish London literary world. Well, our traditional culture hasn't yet been finally reduced, though Snow in his Rede lecture reduces it, to *that*. But his being able to do it quite naturally, without a thought of being questioned, shows where we have got. And the process so exemplified —I permit myself to say what should be obvious—affects the scientist, the scientist as a man, as nearly and intimately as anyone.

I say it, because no one will suggest that *he*, the real scientist (or the technological expert, for that matter), is to be thought of as sharing the state of the human quasi-automaton—the human or animal or organic adjunct to automation. The scientist very well may—the creative kind certainly will—derive great satisfaction from his work. But he cannot derive from it all that a human being needs—intellectually, spiritually, culturally. Yet to think of a distinguished mind having to go for refreshment, edification and nourishment to the 'literary culture' represented by Snow's 'literary intellectual' and identified by Snow with 'the traditional culture' is painful and depressing—unbearably humiliating to some of us. For I was speaking responsibly when I said in my Richmond lecture that Snow's 'literary intellectual' is an enemy of art and life. He belongs to the cultural conditions that make it seem plausible—obvious good sense—to talk about 'The Two Cultures'.

The term 'culture', of course, like most important words, has more forces than one in which it can be used for intellectually respectable purposes; but even if Snow had not with naïve explicitness identified one of his pair with 'the traditional culture', the fair and final dismissing comment on his Rede lecture as offering serious thought about the problem he points to (but doesn't see) would be: 'there is only *one* culture; to talk of *two* in your way is to use an essential term with obviously disqualifying irresponsibility'. It is obviously absurd to posit a 'culture' that the scientist **has** *qua* scientist. What Snow proposes to condemn the scientist to when he points to the really educated man as combining the 'two cultures', what he condemns the scientist to for his cultural needs—his non-scientific *human* needs, is (in the British terms I am familiar with) the culture of the *New Statesman* and the Sunday papers, which is what Snow's 'literary intellectual' actually represents. And for that I have intimated my contempt. No serious problem or theme is being tackled when an alleged 'scientific culture' is being placed against *that* as the complementary reality.

The difficulty about proceeding now on a more positive line is that the issues, being basic, are so large, complex and difficult to limit, and that (a distinctive mark of the present phase of civilization) even in talking to a highly educated audience there is so little one can take as given and granted and understood to be necessarily granted. One can only be clear about one's focal interest and determine one's course and one's economy in relation to that. Mine—ours, may I say?—is the university; that is, the function and the idea.

It may be commented at this point that I am not absolved from explaining what positively I mean by 'culture' in the sense I invoke when I criticize misleading uses of the term. I won't proceed by attempting to offer a direct formal definition; that wouldn't conduce to economy, or to the kind of clarity that for the present purpose we need. Faced with the problem of indicating clearly the nature of my answer to questions about meaning, I recall Snow's account of the supreme creative human achievement present to us in Science, and the comment it moved me to. This is Snow: 'As though the scientific edifice of the physical world', he exclaims, 'were not, in its intellectual depth, complexity and articulation, the most beautiful and wonderful collective work of the mind of man.' My comment was: 'It is pleasant to think of Snow contemplating, daily perhaps, the intellectual depth, complexity and articulation in all their beauty. But there is a prior human achievement of collaborative creation, a more basic work of the mind of man (and more than the mind), one without which the triumphant erection of the scientific edifice would not have been possible: that is, the creation of the human world, including language.'

This is surely a clear enough truth, and I don't suppose anyone here wants to dispute it. The trouble is that in our time, when we need as no other age did before to see that it is given full conscious realizing recognition, there seems to be something like an impossibility of getting anything better than a mere notional assent. Can we without exaggeration say, for instance, that it was even that in the *Guardian* first leader which I read when, a couple of years ago, my thoughts were very much on the theme I am discussing now? The leader, though characteristic enough, a little surprised me, for I had had strong grounds for supposing the *Guardian* pro-Snow and anti-Leavis—committed to the view that there was nothing to be said for my side in the notorious so-called 'debate'. But this leader, dealing with Mr Harold Wilson's 'vision of the future' at Scarborough, remarked that 'even a C. P. Snow would be a poor substitute for an informed and open discussion of the uses to be made of science', and that it 'would . . . be a tragedy if either party gave as its chief reason for a further extension of the universities the need to recruit more scientists'. It concluded: 'Science is a means to an end.'

'Science is a means to an end': what more could one ask?—it concedes everything, doesn't it? You'll reply that 'concedes' is an infelicitous word, the proposition being a truism. Yes, a truism: there's the rub. But 'rub' itself is an infelicitous word: it doesn't—quite the contrary—suggest what I am calling attention to, which is the absence, where 'ends' are adverted to as needing some consideration, of the friction, the sense of pregnant arrest, which goes with active realizing thought and the taking of a real charged meaning. 'Science is a means to an end': yes—a rising standard of living. I perpetrate my notorious exhibition of bad manners at poor Lord Snow's expense, or, as I myself should put it, do my best to get some recognition for the inadequacy of that accepted formula as representing a due concern for human ends (a matter, it seems to me, of great urgency), and I get for response a vast deal of blackguarding, misrepresentation and contemptuous dismissal, and then the *Spectator* offering to strike a *juste milieu* between my Richmond lecture on the one hand, and Aldous Huxley offering to strike a *juste milieu* between me and Snow on the other. The *Spectator*, pointing out how unsatisfactory Huxley is, endorses by making it its own his attribution to me of 'one-track, moralistic literarism'. To set over against Snow's deviation, scientism, you see, there is mine, which is literarism.

I'll leave aside for a moment this curious term, which Huxley, with an American distribution of stress and quantity (after all he, though the *Spectator* challenges for itself with the term the genuine and solid middle position it was meant to claim for him, invented it) found perhaps more speakable than I do. Immediately in place is to insist on the truth—not, unhappily, a truism—that once the naïveté that takes 'rising standard living' to represent an adequate concern for human ends has been trans-cended, the determination of what, adequately conceived, they *are* is seen to be very far from simple. Human nature and need are certainly more complex than Lord

Snow assumes. They won't be fully apparent for recognition in any present of any society. The most carefully analysed and interpreted answers to the most cunningly framed questionnaires, the most searching and thorough sociological surveys, won't yield an adequate account of what they are.

And 'end' itself, though a word that we most certainly have to use in the kind of context and the kind of way I've been exemplifying, tends, perhaps, to turn the receptivity of the mind away from orders of consideration that are essential—essential, that is, when the criteria for determining how we should discriminate and judge in the face of a rapidly changing civilization are what we want to bring to full consciousness. Mankind, for instance, has a need to feel life significant; a hunger for significance that isn't altogether satisfied by devotion to Tottenham Hotspur or by hopes of the World Cup for a team called England or Uruguay, or by space travel (mediated by professional publicists), or by patriotic ardour nourished on international athletics, or by the thrill of broken records—even though records, by dint of scientific training, go on being broken and the measurement of times becomes progressively finer.

If, of course, one is challenged to stand and deliver and say what 'significance' is—'If you use the term you ought to be able to say what you mean by it!'—it is hardly possible to answer convincingly at the level of the challenge. But that is far from saying that the matter for consideration raised with the term is not, when thought turns on human ends, of the greatest moment. And that 'high standard of living' expresses a dangerously inadequate notion or criterion of human prosperity is a simple enough truth.

Now, if we are asked how we are to arrive—for our-selves, in the first place, but of course, not merely that—at a more adequate notion, the answer, it seems to me, clearly is: when human ends require to be pondered in relation to the pressing problems and opportunities with which our civilization faces us, one's thinking should not be blind to the insights given in cultural tradition—on the contrary, it should be informed with the knowledge of basic human need that is transmitted by *that*. This is not a simple answer; no serious answer *could* be. I have used the phrase 'cultural tradition' rather than Snow's 'the traditional culture', because this last suggests some-thing quite different from what I mean. It suggests something belonging to the past, a reservoir of alleged wisdom, an established habit, an unadventurousness in the face of life and change. Let me, as against that, extend briefly the quotation I've permitted myself from my Richmond lecture. Having, in comment on Snow's claim regarding the 'scientific edifice of the physical world', pointed to the 'prior human achievement of collaborative creation . . . the creation of the human world, including language', I go on: 'It is one we cannot rest on as on something done in the past. It lives in the living creative response to change in the present.' A little further on, insisting on the antithesis to what 'traditional' usually suggests, I put it in this way, and the formulation gives me what I need now: 'for the sake of our humanity —our humanness, for the sake of a human future we must do, with intelligent resolution and with faith, all we can to maintain the full life in the present—and life is growth—of our transmitted culture'.

We have no other; there is only one, and there can be no substitute. Those who talk of two and of joining them would present us impressively with the sum of two nothings: it is the void the modern world tackles with drugs, sex and alcohol.[1] That kind of sage doesn't touch on the real problem; he has no cognizance of it. It is a desperately difficult problem; I don't pretend to know of comfortable answers and easy solutions. Simply I believe that in respect of this problem, too, intelligence-directed human effort has *its* part to play, and that there is a human instinct of self-preservation to be appealed to.

In my Richmond lecture, recalling a formulation I had been prompted to in the old days, when the Marxising expositors of human affairs thronged the arena, I remarked that there is a certain autonomy of the human spirit. I didn't mean by that to suggest that the higher non-material achievements of human culture, the achievements of collaborative creation that belong most obviously to what I call in discussion the 'third realm', were to be thought of as spontaneous, unconditioned expressions of an intrinsic human nature sprouting or creating gratuitously, in a realm of pure spirit. I was merely insisting that there *is* an intrinsic human nature, with needs and latent potentialities the most brilliant scientist may very well be blank about, and the technologically-directed planner may ignore—with (it doesn't need arguing) disastrous consequences. Of course, the collaborative creation of the world of significances and values has to be seen as a matter of response to material conditions and economic necessities.

Let me repeat, however, that I didn't thirty years ago point to the state of affairs, the relation between cultural values (or—shall I say?—human significances) and

[1] And, I can now add, 'student unrest' and the vote and majority-status at eighteen.

economic fact, documented in *The Wheelwright's Shop*—
which I've hardly mentioned these thirty years—as
something we should aim at recovering; but as something
finally gone. That relation was an essential condition of
the kind of achievement of the higher culture (spiritual,
intellectual, humane) that is represented by Shakespeare's
works. Such a relation, for any world we can foresee, is
gone.

Technological change has marked cultural consequences. There is an implicit logic that will impose, if
not met by creative intelligence and corrective purpose,
simplifying and reductive criteria of human need and
human good, and generate, to form the mind and spirit
of civilization, disastrously false and inadequate conceptions of the *ends* to which science should be a means.
This logic or drive is immensely and insidiously powerful.
Its tendency appears very plainly in the cultural effects
of mass-production—in the levelling-down that goes with
standardization. Ponder, I find myself saying in England,
to academic audiences, the 'magazine sections' of the
Sunday papers (they know which two I mean), and tell
yourselves that *this*, for many dons—and I am thinking
of the non-scientists, the custodians of culture—represents
the top level: what Arnold meant by 'the best that is
thought and known in our time'. It will almost certainly
represent the top level for those who, at this time of rapid
and confident and large scale reforms, make the authoritative and decisive recommendations in the field of higher
education.

To point out these things is not to be a Luddite. It is
to insist on the truth that, in an age of revolutionary and
constantly advancing technology, the sustained collaborative devotion of directed energy and directing intelligence

that is science needs to be accompanied by another, and quite different, devotion of purpose and energy, another sustained collaborative effort of creative intelligence. I will again quote what I actually said in the offending lecture: 'the advance of science and technology means a human future of change so rapid and of such kinds, of tests and challenges so unprecedented, of decisions and possible non-decisions so momentous and insidious in their consequences, that mankind—this is surely clear— will need to be in full intelligent possession of its full humanity. . . . What we need, and shall continue to need not less, is something with the livingness of the deepest vital instinct; as intelligence, a power—rooted, strong in experience, and supremely human—of creative response to the new challenges of time; something that is alien to both of Snow's cultures.'

What I have been pointing out is that we shall not have this power if provision is not made for a more conscious and deliberate fostering of it than has characterized our civilization in the past. And here comes in my concern for the idea of the university as a focus of consciousness and human responsibility.

I must close on the note of transition, for I can't here follow up this opening. My mention of the idea of the university is a concluding emphasis on the positive; an insistence that my attitude is very much a positive one, and that I *have* a positive theme for the development of which I am fully charged—a theme intent on practice. Of course, I speak—have been speaking (that was plain— and was expected of me)—as an Englishman, and my 'engaged' preoccupation with the idea of the university has a British context, the tight little island of Mr Harold Wilson's premiership and Lord Robbins's Report on

Higher Education. Yet I can't think of the differences between the situation I face at home in England and the situation in America (which, as I've remarked, is not a tight little island) without telling myself with conviction that we face in essence one and the same problem, and that the widest community of the intelligently concerned that can be made aware of itself and of the menace will not be too large. I have reason for knowing, with encouragement and gratitude,—that there are many Americans who feel the same.

The special bent of my positive concern is given when I gloss 'the university as a focus of consciousness and human responsibility' by 'the university as a guarantor of a real performance of the critical function—that critical function which is a creative one'. It is here, of course, that I am supposed to have laid myself open to the charge of 'literarism'—for it is obviously meant to be a charge. Its suggestion is very much that of the writer in the *Melbourne Quarterly* who, in a quite flattering article, said I sometimes seem to think that literary criticism will save us. The possibility of this irony meaning anything seems to depend on a conception of literary criticism that, when I try, I can't conceive—it eludes me.

For—and this is my reply to Aldous Huxley as well— I don't believe in any 'literary values', and you won't find me talking about them; the judgments the literary critic is concerned with are judgments about life. What the critical discipline is concerned with is relevance and precision in making and developing them. To think that to have a vital contemporary performance of the critical function matters is to think that creative literature matters; and it matters because to have a living literature, a literary tradition that *lives* in the present—and nothing

23

lives unless it goes on being creative, is to have, as an informing spirit in civilization, an informed, charged and authoritative awareness of inner human nature and human need.

In my discussions of the university English School as a liaison centre I have been intent on enforcing my conviction as to the kind of effort by which we must promote the growth of that power of which I have just spoken: 'a power—rooted, strong in experience and supremely human—of creative response to the new challenges of time; something that is alien to both of Snow's cultures'. My concern for the idea of an English School isn't to be thought of as just a matter of syllabus, teaching methods and a given kind of student product to be turned out. The educational problem itself in that narrow sense conduces to discouragement, despair and cynicism when approached merely in those terms.

But I won't now develop that observation beyond saying that one's essential concern should conceive itself as being to make the university what it ought to be—something (that is) more than a collocation of specialist departments: a centre of consciousness for the community. The problem is to re-establish an effective educated public, for it is only in the existence of an educated public, capable of responding and making its response felt, that 'standards' can be there for the critic to appeal to. This is true not merely of literary criticism; the literary-critical judgment is the type of all judgments and valuations belonging to what in my unphilosophical way I've formed the habit of calling the 'third realm'— the collaboratively created human world, the realm of what is *neither* public in the sense belonging to science (it can't be weighed or tripped over or brought into the

24

laboratory or pointed to) *nor* merely private and personal (consider the nature of a language, of the language we can't do without—and literature is a manifestation of language). One's aim is that the university itself, having a real and vital centre of consciousness, should *be* such a public or community as the critic needs, being in that way one of the sustaining creative nuclei of a larger community.

One might then hope that one might, at Cambridge, for example—my own university (and Lord Snow's and Lord Annan's)—get the effective response when one uttered the appropriate judgment on the publicizers, public relations men, heads of houses, academic ward-bosses, hobnobbers with Cabinet ministers, who are planning, they tell us, to remodel the University and start going a new kind of higher education. Might . . . might, if . . . if . . .; but don't take me to be suggesting that the actuality and the blind enlightened menace are anything but what they are. Let me end with a sentence and a bit from Lord Robbins of the Robbins Report:

> Since Sir Charles Snow's Rede lecture, we have heard a great deal of the two cultures in this country; for reasons which I completely fail to understand, Sir Charles's very moderate indication of danger arouses very high passions. To me his diagnosis seems obvious. . . .

To me it seems obvious that Snow's *raison d'être* is to be an elementary test.

2
Eliot's Classical Standing

ELIOT'S CLASSICAL STANDING

As I was beginning on the draft of this lecture I received a copy of a recent essay on Eliot by a critic who had become aware of him as a poet at much the same time as I had—that is, in the very early 'twenties—and who, though politically Left-inclined, wrote in the *Criterion*. In the essay he says, referring to *The Waste Land*: 'We met Eliot first in his most demanding, and, I still think his most impressive, work.' Those judgments seem to me untenable, and essentially what I aim at doing in this lecture is to explain in what ways, and to what effect, I disagree with them. We rightly found *The Waste Land* very impressive and very important in the 1920s, but I think we tended to make it a higher kind of achievement than it actually is. And we didn't, in the 1920s, foresee— no one *could*—the impressive kind of thing his total achievement would be seen to be when we should have the whole creative work there before us. Perhaps I had better be more modest, or affirmative, and say, the kind of thing *I* now see it to be.

The essayist, at the beginning of his essay, says that of the three poets, Hardy, Yeats and Eliot, 'Eliot, though perhaps the least in stature, was nevertheless the most influential.' I myself think that before the death of either of the others it ought to have been plain that Eliot was the greatest. The testimony that he was the most *influential* is of course well-founded, and here we have an order of consideration that I want to eliminate as much as possible from my own particular approach. Eliot was a decisive influence on taste and critical fashion. And this last head, 'critical fashion', is not as narrowly definitive as the phrase might at first suggest. There was the play of political opinion and attitude that characterized the literary climate—Eliot himself (modestly) called attention to Mirsky's essay, 'T. S. Eliot et la fin de la poésie bourgeoise', as an important document. There were Fascism, and Communism, and Action Française, and Anglo-Catholicism, and Classicism—and there was literary coterie. 'Influential', that is, calls attention to a number of things that a critic—or the editor of a critical journal—couldn't in the 1930s ignore. They are not my business now. I think the time has come when they can be got out of the way of the strictly critical effort; I mean, that which asks: 'What can we now see the distinctive nature of Eliot's creative effort to be—what has he left as pure, significant, achieved creation, qualified (that is) to exercise the profoundest kind of influence?

I have made it plain already that the answer I find irresistible assigns to the poet a very high place. I see Eliot's creative career as a sustained, heroic and indefatigably resourceful quest of a profound sincerity of the most difficult kind. The heroism is that of genius. The poetic technique of his intense preoccupation *is* a technique for sincerity—consciously that at any rate from 'The Hollow Men' onwards. He would not, I think, have said—in that least agreeable of his ironic modes— of anything in that poem or *Ash-Wednesday* or the *Ariel* poems, that, while exegetists had found deep significance in this phrase or line or passage, he had actually put it in because he liked the sound of it.

Having attributed heroism to Eliot and said that

poetic technique for him is a technique for sincerity in relation to the most difficult personal strains (I put it this way now), I can't avoid some reference to the *paradox*: I mean, that represented by his 'classicism', of which D. H. Lawrence said (justly, I think): 'this classiosity is bunkum; still more cowardice'. He was thinking of 'Tradition and the Individual Talent', the famous essay in which Eliot tries—for the purpose is essentially that—to absolve the artist from responsibility towards life.

'Someone said: "The dead writers are remote from us because we know so much more than they did." Precisely, and they are that which we know.' One can imagine contexts in which that affirmation, that emphasis, might be respectable, but it has no such context in Eliot's essay. The essay is incoherent, self-contradictory and equivocal, but the spirit of it is plain. It is the spirit that avows itself in Eliot's exaltation of Landor, of whom he says in another place that Landor is a test of whether you go to poetry because it is poetry you are interested in, or merely in order to have your own feeble lusts and desires flattered.

'Tradition and the Individual Talent', I said, is incoherent. Its interest and significance are diagnostic. Now, as I've tried to make clear, diagnosis is the kind of thing that in this lecture I want to concern myself with as little as possible, We must, however, at least touch on peculiarities of personal make-up, we can't altogether avoid diagnostic considerations, when concerned to define his essential interest and clear the way for a constatation of what, creatively, the poet achieved. We ask what leads him to find such felicity in that analogical play with the catalyst, and we ponder that odd account of the creative process: 'The poet's mind is in fact a receptacle for seizing and storing up numberless feelings, phrases, images, which remain there till all the particles which can unite to form a new compound are present together.'

'Are present', 'can unite', 'new compound'—wait duly, and that, it seems, is poetic creation; we are absolved from asking any questions about the creative energy, what it is and where it comes from. The possibility that one might still ask does in fact get some kind of recognition in the next sentence but one: 'For it is not the "greatness", the intensity, of the emotions, the components, but the intensity of the artistic process, the pressure, so to speak, under which the fusion takes place, that counts.' The casually interpolated word 'pressure', which gets no development or commentary, and no support from the context, gives the clue. Eliot doesn't need to think about the 'pressure' in relation to his own artistic 'intensities', and he has a deep-seated habit of *not* thinking about it, and of *not* bringing it into focus for clear, conscious recognition. Why this should be so is explained by the light thrown on it in the essay on *Hamlet* of much the same date. We read there of the disgust—bearing on sex, of course—which constitutes Hamlet's 'bafflement' (and Shakespeare's too, we are told in an equivocal way). 'It is thus a feeling which he cannot understand; he cannot objectify it, and it therefore remains to poison life and obstruct action.'

We note that Eliot doesn't doubt that *he* knows sufficiently what kind of experience Shakespeare's play does after all communicate—and we know from Eliot's own poetry that the disgust that constitutes so large a part of the 'pressure' in his own creativity as poet is something that poisons life—just as it makes it impossible for him to think coherently as a critic when he offers to discuss the nature of poetic creation. He says in a once 'influential' dictum—which can't have influenced anything but quasi-intellectual fashion: 'the more perfect the artist, the more completely separate in him will be the man who suffers and the mind which creates'. The relevant truth, the clear essential truth, is stated when one reverses the dictum and says that between the man who suffers and the mind which creates there can never be a separation.

It was because there so clearly wasn't one in Eliot's poetry contemporaneous with the essay that he was recognized at once, or should have been, as a poet of rare gift. Here, unmistakably, was a creative mind, however paradoxically so—I am thinking, of course, of the part played in the 'pressure' by disgust and revulsion and of the complex intensity of personal emotion avowed, with discreet irony, in the epigraph of 'Sweeney among the Nightingales':

ὤμοι πέπληγμαι καιρίαν πληγὴν ἔσω

The poem of Eliot's I read first, unless my memory deceives me, was 'The Love Song of J. Alfred Prufrock'. It comes first in the *Collected Poems* but I read it in the very early 'twenties, having found it in some anthology of American verse. Ever since, phrases and lines and even a longer passage or two have lodged in my mind. For me they recall the effect of the whole context, the disconcerting impressiveness of the poem. The qualities that made it impressive and memorable seem to me, however, better discussed in terms of the closely related finer poem, 'Portrait of a Lady', also from *Prufrock* (1917). It is a poem that, in pursuit of my present purpose, which is to convey a given sense of Eliot's creative achievement, its

33

form, its ethos, its graph (so to speak), I want to put a star against. 'Sensibility alters from generation to generation in everybody, whether we will or no, but expression is only altered by a man of genius': everybody now knows that sentence from one of Eliot's best essays. With 'Portrait of a Lady' in front of one, oughtn't one to find oneself saying, with the completest conviction: 'But already by 1917 this young poet had effectively "altered expression" '? Much, one should in (say) 1920 have been able to see, must follow a poetic success of this kind, though no one could have foreseen the actual development.

I mustn't forget that I have only a short hour, but I must halt at the poem long enough to disown firmly what possibly seemed the general implication of my comments on some of Eliot's best-known criticism. Best-known, but not best: his best criticism, which does indeed give him a distinguished place among critics, comes from the poet who was 'conscious enough' (his own word and phrase) to be, around 1920, successfully 'altering expression'.

I will read the middle section of the poem:

> *Now that lilacs are in bloom*
> *She has a bowl of lilacs in her room*
> *And twists one in her fingers while she talks.*
> *'Ah, my friend, you do not know, you do not know*
> *What life is, you who hold it in your hands';*
> *(Slowly twisting the lilac stalks)*
> *'You let it flow from you, you let it flow,*
> *And youth is cruel, and has no remorse*
> *And smiles at situations which it cannot see.'*
> *I smile, of course,*
> *And go on drinking tea.*

34

'Yet with these April sunsets, that somehow recall
My buried life, and Paris in the Spring,
I feel immeasurably at peace, and find the world
To be wonderful and youthful, after all.'

The voice returns like the insistent out-of-tune
Of a broken violin on an August afternoon:
'I am always sure that you understand
My feelings, always sure that you feel,
Sure that across the gulf you reach your hand.

You are invulnerable, you have no Achilles' heel.
You will go on, and when you have prevailed
You can say: at this point many a one has failed.
But what have I, but what have I, my friend,
To give you, what can you receive from me?
Only the friendship and the sympathy
Of one about to reach her journey's end.

I shall sit here, serving tea to friends. . . .'

I take my hat: how can I make a cowardly amends
For what she has said to me?
You will see me any morning in the park
Reading the comics and the sporting page.
Particularly I remark
An English countess goes upon the stage.
A Greek was murdered at a Polish dance,
Another bank defaulter has confessed.
I keep my countenance,
I remain self-possessed
Except when a street piano, mechanical and tired
Reiterates some worn-out common song

With the smell of hyacinths across the garden
Recalling things that other people have desired.
Are these ideas right or wrong?

It is hard to realize now how remarkable and significant this was—should have been seen to be—in the
early 1920s. One might ask what difficulty it presented
to the educated public of that time. No intrinsic difficulty,
clearly; and the affront to the reader's habits of expectation was surely not violent (as it might in various ways
be said to have been in, say, 'Sweeney Erect' or even
'Gerontion'). The poem might reasonably, in those days
of Free Verse and Imagism, have been called 'traditional'.
The rhythmic life is irresistible, and must have been
felt to be so at any time.

But when I speak of 'rhythmic life' it is the essential
characteristics of the poem that are really in question—
the characteristics that make it something new in poetic
art and, in a vital way, positively and decisively post-
Victorian. For in that life, which is both strong and
subtle, of the rhythm the changing subtleties of the tone
clearly play a large part. And though the word 'tone'
suggests something vague and indeterminate, what it
should lead us on to take note of is in fact quite other.
For the delicate play of shifting tone that is essential to
the theme and communication of the poem is a matter
of appealing to the reader's sense of how things go
naturally. And the poet can command such a play only
in a medium that can suggest (as a Miltonic or Tenny-
sonian or Swinburnian medium cannot) the subtleties of
living speech—make the reader, that is, recall them
appropriately with precision and delicacy.

With this use of language goes a new freedom of access
to experience and a closeness to its actual texture, together with a flexibility of tone inconceivable in serious
poetry ('genuine poetry') while the Arnoldian canons prevailed—as they did unchallenged when I was at school.

You will see me any morning in the park
Reading the comics and the sporting page

— the context is not satire or 'light verse': within a few lines we have, by an inevitable transition:

Except when a street piano, mechanical and tired
Re-iterates some worn-out common song
With the smell of hyacinths across the garden
Recalling things that other people have desired.
Are these ideas right or wrong?

—which is both poignant and more concentrated and subtle than anything we could find in Victorian poetry. And

how can I make a cowardly amends
For what she has said to me?

—Wit? You see, the full waking attention is demanded— is compelled—in this use of language and rhythm.

I will continue this very obvious commentary no further. I've said enough—and I hope I've said not much more than enough—for my purpose, which is to insist on the nature and distinction of Eliot's best criticism, to do which is to constate the actual relation between that criticism and his poetry.

I find it exasperating that the critical achievement in which his genius is so magnificently effective should have so little intelligent appreciation, while such things as 'Tradition and the Individual Talent' and the British Academy lecture on Milton are overrated and acclaimed. He did *not* 'recant' about Milton; he merely contrived a discourse in which, while actually (to do him justice) he conceded nothing, but confirmed the judgments he had made earlier with such economy, he enabled his audience to *feel* that he had recanted. How clear he was in his own

37

mind about what he was doing I don't know (there are penalties for expertness in that art), but he knew he *couldn't* recant about Milton without repudiating his genius and his *raison d'être*.

That his essays on poetry in the seventeenth century had an immense influence is accepted commonplace. The modish academic attitude towards them has been for a good while now, I've observed, to be 'appreciative' and superior, with an irony directed against critics who suppose that Eliot made any valid suggestion about a momentous change occurring in the seventeenth century —any suggestion that had, and deserved to have, a great influence on critical thought and the understanding of English history. I don't myself favour attempts to justify the phrase, 'dissociation of sensibility', systematically with a show of analytic precision. Such attempts aren't worth while. The phrase as Eliot uses it prompts no such development; it serves its purpose quite well in the context Eliot gives it, and he makes plain enough to anyone interested in poetry what the use and the purpose are. The three essays reprinted together in the Hogarth pamphlet, *Homage to John Dryden*, were the outcome of journalistic occasions admirably taken—taken with such effect because Eliot was charged with relevant interests and preoccupations. In discussing the Metaphysical poets and Marvell and Dryden he calls attention to the consequences in poetic history of the great total change that was seen in the Restoration period to have been accomplished in civilization—in ethos, in intellectual habit, and in the English language. With a fine tact of intelligence very different from the mode of 'Tradition and the Individual Talent' he calls attention to qualities that are not to be found in English poetry of the nineteenth century—qualities *excluded* by the habits and assumptions implicit in the axiom: 'genuine poetry is conceived and composed in the soul'.

The qualities are those which in 'Portrait of a Lady' account for the failure of that poem, which presents no intellectual difficulty, and no difficulty of theme, convention or organization, to get itself promptly recognized as the work of a highly gifted poet.

I want to pass on from it to a very different poem, 'La figlia che piange', which is short enough to read in full, but is very important, at any rate for my purpose, which entails by-passing *The Waste Land*. It too appeared in *Prufrock*. I must first however, very briefly, say something about the difference between Eliot's best criticism—his best prose—and the rest; between the essay on Marvell on the one hand and, on the other, 'Tradition and the Individual Talent' and the British Academy lecture on Milton. These last two differ from each other in their kinds of badness, but the badness in both exemplifies the truth that Eliot's intelligence, Eliot's insight, doesn't show to advantage in the social world; the gifts that make him important to us don't function in that climate. 'Social world', I know, is not a sharply definitive expression, but I don't think I need spend time over shades and transitions of meaning.

. . . I have seen the eternal Footman hold my coat and snicker
And in short, I was afraid.

—That is J. Alfred Prufrock. One wouldn't have hit on the word 'afraid' for the notability addressing the British Academy—or the University of Virginia, but he was certainly concerned to impress favourably an audience, or an element in his audience, whose opinion the essential great poet, and those capable of recognizing the distinction of his work, would have despised. In 'Tradition and the Individual Talent' the case is of a rather subtler kind. The attitudinizing and confused intellectuality to which his inner insecurity (or fear) impels him are implicitly addressed to the intellectual coterie-world in which he has been formed. The same is true of the element of exhibitionistic sophistication to be found in his early verse.

I repeat, I take no pleasure in the diagnostic note. What I am intent on is justifying my attribution to Eliot of a heroic quality in the exercise of his genius—the genius that expresses itself in the way in which, for him, poetic technique became a technique for achieving and sustaining a most difficult sincerity. 'Became'—I am insisting on the fact of development. And no one need suppose I am implicitly judging the early poetry to be *in*sincere. Of 'La figlia che piange' (1917), from which, in my preoccupation with the nature of the development, I want (but for a by-the-way glance at 'The Hollow Men') to pass straight to *Ash-Wednesday*, no one would judge that it didn't come from somewhere very deep in Eliot.

By-passing, I said, *The Waste Land*—a necessary measure of economy which, my special preoccupation being what it is, I see no reason for being uneasy about. That poem, with its marvellous display of rhythmic mastery and its diversity of poetic life, offers no real difficulty. We were right in the 1920s to be immensely impressed by it and to see it as an important event; but I think we attributed to it a higher status as an organic work than it deserves. Eliot's rapid acceptance as a major creative power was associated with the belief that the poem *was* what it offered itself as being: an achieved and representatively significant work—significance here being something to be discussed in terms of the bankruptcy of civilization, the 'modern consciousness', the 'modern sense of the human situation', *la condition humaine*, and so on. Well, Eliot was born and brought up in the modern world and *The Waste Land* is full of references to it. But for all the use of Fraser and of fertility-ritual allusions, the treatment of the theme of the dried-up springs and the failure of life hasn't the breadth of significance claimed and asserted by the title and the apparatus of notes. The distinctive attitude towards, the feeling about, the relations between men and women that predominates in the poem is the highly personal one we know so well from the earlier poems; the symbolic Waste Land makes itself felt too much as Thomas Stearns Eliot's.

'La figlia che piange' doesn't pretend to be anything but lyrically personal, but the feeling is different.

Stand on the highest pavement of the stair—
Lean on a garden urn—
Weave, weave the sunlight in your hair—
Clasp your flowers to you with a pained surprise—
Fling them to the ground and turn
With a fugitive resentment in your eyes:
But weave, weave the sunlight in your hair.

So I would have had him leave,
So I would have had her stand and grieve,
So he would have left
As the soul leaves the body torn and bruised,
As the mind deserts the body it has used.
I should find
Some way incomparably light and deft,
Some way we both should understand,
Simple and faithless as a smile and shake of the hand.

She turned away, but with the autumn weather
Compelled my imagination many days,
Many days and many hours:
Her hair over her arms and her arms full of flowers.
And I wonder how they should have been together!
I should have lost a gesture and a pose.
Sometimes these cogitations still amaze
The troubled midnight and the noon's repose.

Love—love in the lyrical sense, with no irony in the tone or context: where else in Eliot do you find that? The general, and pregnant, truth about him is that he can contemplate the relations between men and women only with revulsion or distaste—unless with the aid of Dante. *The Waste Land* offers us a comprehensive survey of the well-springs, the sources of life (which have failed), but the only presence of love is this, where love is romantically-nostalgically evoked:

Frisch weht der Wind
Der Heimat zu
Mein Irisch Kind,
Wo weilest du?

'You gave me hyacinths first a year ago;
They called me the hyacinth girl?'
—Yet, when we came back late from the hyacinth
   garden,
Your arms full, and your hair wet, I could not
Speak, and my eyes failed, I was neither
Living nor dead, and I knew nothing,
Looking into the heart of light, the silence.

Oed' und leer das Meer.

Love: that what we have in 'La figlia che piange' is something that comes under that head no one I think will question. The implicit dramatic situation is in one sense indeterminate (just what was the poet's part in it?), but the essential definition, the definition of the quality of the memory, is perfect. For when in connexion with a poem of Eliot's one talks of a 'memory' one can have no tendency to think of 'memories' as imprints (of the nature, say, of snapshots) preserved from the past in some repository where they have lain inert and, but for fading, unchanged. In 'La figlia che piange' the memory is the poem, and the poem is a product of the poet's creative power, but clearly has nothing arbitrary about it and is not 'imaginative' in any sense that doesn't imply a more than ordinary responsibility. The poem is unique, but the memory obviously represents something very important for Eliot, some vital node of experience—something felt as perhaps a possibility of transcending disgust, rejection and protest. We know this not just from the power of the poem itself, but from the part played by closely related evocations in his later poetry.

The poem I shall now read from comes from a dozen years later (I read it first, along with a French translation *en regard*, in a very *chic* French organ, under the title 'Som de l'escalina'—which of course is a phrase from that Provençal passage spoken by Arnaut Daniel in the *Purgatorio*):

> *At the first turning of the second stair*
> *I turned and saw below*
> *The same shape twisted on the banister*
> *Under the vapour in the fetid air*
> *Struggling with the devil of the stairs who wears*
> *The deceitful face of hope and of despair.*
>
> *At the second turning of the second stair*
> *I left them twisting, turning below;*

There were no more faces and the stair was dark,
Damp, jaggèd, like an old man's mouth drivelling, beyond
  repair,
Or the toothed gullet of an agèd shark.

At the first turning of the third stair
Was a slotted window bellied like the fig's fruit
And beyond the hawthorn blossom and a pasture scene
The broadbacked figure drest in blue and green
Enchanted the maytime with an antique flute.
Blown hair is sweet, brown hair over the mouth blown,
Lilac and brown hair;
Distraction, music of the flute, stops and steps of the mind
  over the third stair,
Fading, fading . . .

About the sense in which *Ash-Wednesday* is religious poetry I shall have to try and say something. The point I want to make immediately is that the way in which the poem I have just read relates to 'La figlia' who

> *turned away, but with the autumn weather*
> *Compelled my imagination many days,*
> *Many days and many hours,*
> *Her hair over her arms and her arms full of flowers*

is clearly a vital one. Reading 'Som de l'escalina' immediately after the earlier poem we see a deeper significance in

> *Sometimes these cogitations still amaze*
> *The troubled midnight and the noon's repose*

—the close of the earlier. The prelude to *Ash-Wednesday* is the phase of 'The Hollow Men', a poem in which there is no protest, no irony and no contemptuous revulsion, except from the self to which there is implicitly imputed something like guilt for a failure in itself.

44

The Eliot of 'The Hollow Men' had a desperate need to be able to believe in, to be sure of, something real not himself that should claim allegiance and give meaning. A quest driven by such a need inevitably became consciously religious, and *Ash-Wednesday* is clearly that. 'Som de l'escalina' makes plain the part played in the poet's struggle to escape from 'death's twilight kingdom' by 'cogitations' turning on the 'memory' or inherent in it. Love, human love, an intense and deep-lying and cherished experience coming under that head and become an established emotional centre or spiritual value (some such expression has to be used)—that for the poet lost in the 'dead land' appears as the intimation, or gleam, of a reality to be sought with disciplined devotion.

What admirers of *Ash-Wednesday* tend to misrepresent is the nature of the discipline that makes it, with the poetry that follows, so extraordinary an achievement. It is when we come to *Ash-Wednesday* that there is point in saying that poetic technique for Eliot here is a technique for sincerity. He makes no religious affirmation; even what might seem to be his implicit affirmations of belief or acceptance are made by their total context expressions of a spirit, and contributory to an effect, that could hardly exalt or reassure most of the admirers of *The Rock* or *The Murder in the Cathedral*. And here again I come to the distinction between the creative genius and the Eliot who can't escape from his consciousness of the social world, and who forgets that what really matters most to him doesn't belong there. One would hardly think of calling the religious plays insincere; but the difficult and rare kind of sincerity in question is *not* to be attributed to them.

Eliot in *Ash-Wednesday* is concerned to discover, by a

tentative, exploratory, and wholly unwilful kind of creativeness, scrupulously unassertive, what assurance, what reality, what that can be set against the experience of 'death's twilight kingdom', he may hope to establish as the significance portended by the hints and gleams and elusive apprehensions. Of course, the sensibility is without any disguise Christian. But the insistent liturgical element and the so much else that bears out the avowal of the title don't make Eliot anything but a very different kind of poet from Herbert; the comment on them will express one's sense that his power of achieving an almost impossible sincerity is truly astonishing:

> The Lady is withdrawn
> In a white gown, to contemplation, in a white gown.
> Let the whiteness of bones alone to forgetfulness.
> There is no life in them. As I am forgotten
> And would be forgotten, so I would forget
> Thus devoted, concentrated in purpose. And God said
> Prophesy to the wind, to the wind only for only
> The wind will listen. And the bones sang chirping
> With the burden of the grasshopper . . .

We have here, of course, only a very small part of the whole complex and utterly unproselike play, defying paraphrase, of diverse impulsion, nisus and constatation that *Ash-Wednesday* is. 'Thus devoted, concentrated in purpose'—the paradoxical felicity might serve as an epigraph for the whole work, to do a close analytic study of which would be to illustrate the felicity, while bringing out how completely the 'purpose' that expresses itself in *Ash-Wednesday* entails an abeyance of directing will and idea, and how impossible it would be to summarize the upshot, in terms of acceptance and belief, of that complex play, that quasi-musical organization.

I will now, having made a few preliminary observations, read a short poem that in the collected volume is assigned to the same year, but in first publication came just after *Ash-Wednesday*: 'Marina', a favourite of mine. You will note—you will have noted before—how the various images and evoked memories and associations are, without being linked in any prose-like way, brought together and made to co-operate in the evocation of a significant order of reality that, in the face of transience and death, offers hope and promise—not Yeats's 'Byzantium', with its ironical equivocalness, but, if elusive, unironically so, and truly a hope. The key association is given in the title, Marina being the daughter in Shakespeare's *Pericles*, the daughter who was lost and is found, a promise of continued life—life felt as both personal and impersonal—in the face of inevitable death. The tone of questioning exploring, enchanted wonder is that which comes out in something like statement towards the close:

The awakened, lips parted, the hope, the new ships.

And the foil is the passage evoking death. The element of constructive effort ('Having to construct something upon which to rejoice') is given in 'I made this . . .'

What seas what shores what grey rocks and what islands
What water lapping the bow
And scent of pine and the woodthrush singing through the fog
What images return
O my daughter.

Those who sharpen the tooth of the dog, meaning
Death
Those who glitter with the glory of the hummingbird, meaning
Death
Those who sit in the stye of contentment, meaning
Death

Those who suffer the ecstasy of the animals, meaning
Death

   Are become unsubstantial, reduced by a wind,
A breath of pine, and the woodsong fog
By this grace dissolved in place

   What is this face, less clear and clearer
The pulse in the arm, less strong and stronger—
Given or lent? more distant than stars and nearer than the eye

   Whispers and small laughter between leaves and hurrying
     feet
Under sleep, where all the waters meet.

   Bowsprit cracked with ice and paint cracked with heat.
I made this, I have forgotten
And remember.
The rigging weak and the canvas rotten
Between one June and another September.
Made this unknowing, half conscious, unknown, my own.
The garboard strake leaks, the seams need caulking.
This form, this face, this life
Living to live in a world of time beyond me; let me
Resign my life for this life, my speech for that unspoken,
The awakened, lips parted, the hope, the new ships.

   What seas what shores what granite islands towards my
     timbers
And woodthrush calling through the fog
My daughter.

There is nothing liturgical here, and the only specifically Christian suggestion is in that word 'grace':

   By this grace dissolved in place.

But, for all the differences, the preoccupation and the exploratory-creative procedure are essentially those of *Ash-Wednesday.*

48

By passing from *Ash-Wednesday* to 'Marina' in this way I have of course meant to convey my not singular or (I imagine) generally surprising judgment that one doesn't need to be an Anglo-Catholic, or theologically given, to find a compelling interest and a validity (the 'interest' entails a response to *that*) in Eliot's religious poetry.

To recognize a validity, however, doesn't preclude an attitude of 'Yes, but—'. One's very indebtedness to the authors to whom one is most indebted is commonly in some measure a matter of their compelling one to a convinced 'but'. And 'Marina', with its unliturgical and un-Dantean human tenderness, leads me to remark once more that Eliot seems never to have been able to take cognizance of full human love between the sexes.

> *What images return*
> *O my daughter*

—that is surprisingly, and touchingly, less remote than anything in *Ash-Wednesday* or *Four Quartets* but (a tribute to Shakespeare's power) it is unique, and, in general, the relations between man and woman implied by the 'daughter' don't, for the poet, exist. Yet love in the full sense, the creative relation between the sexes in all its significance, should surely have been of supreme importance to a poet of Eliot's preoccupation. But

> *The Lady is withdrawn*
> *In a white gown, to contemplation, in a white gown*

—the significance that tells for Eliot is that figured in Dante and Beatrice. And I will risk saying crudely that in relation to his own quest, Eliot overvalued what Dante had to offer him; he might have got from Shakespeare, or there was to be got, a great deal that Dante couldn't

49

give—a great deal more than is represented by that resonance from *Pericles*.

The fact is that his inner disorder and his disability remained grievous and tell to its disadvantage on his concern for the spiritual. This comes out with embarrassing clarity in the plays—the theatre plays, which belong of course to the social world, where his heroic sincerity disappears, however much needed for the given undertaking. I can best make the point by quoting a brief passage from D. W. Harding, who is more sympathetic to the Eliot I don't like than I am. Discussing *The Cocktail Party* he writes:

> Reilly's [the psychiatrist's] handling of the Chamberlaynes is one with the slight complacency, the knowledgeableness about spiritual things, that spoils the tone of some of the agents' speeches and arises partly from the hints of their undefined affiliation with higher powers. Obviously Eliot wished to keep alive a suggestion of the supernatural all through the play, and to fuse it with the mundane manipulations—telegrams to reassemble the cocktail party and so forth—that an ordinary detective agency could have managed. The danger is of a slight cheapness creeping in. It is hard, for instance, to see a serious purpose in Reilly's account of his original intuition (expressed in an apparition) that Celia was destined to a violent death. It seems beside the point; the significance of her choice was unconnected with the kind of death to which she was on her way. . . .

You'll find a great deal more that's relevant in the essay, which I recommend to you along with the book: *Experience into Words*.

But—'the danger is of a slight cheapness creeping in': I find something worse than that; or to put it another way, my reaction is more decided. Harding makes, with what is to me a surprising indulgence, his observation that obviously Eliot wished to keep alive a suggestion of the supernatural all through the play. That kind of resort to the 'supernatural' in such a context is both indefensible and betraying: it reveals in Eliot an inner pressure towards the worst kind of insincerity, that which is unconscious. If one admitted as respectable and possibly helpful a use of the term 'supernatural' in the serious discussion of spiritual values that Eliot's poetry both prompts and nourishes, the provocation, or occasion, would be a very different kind of thing. And when anyone used the term, I personally should find myself looking with some intensity into what he might mean by 'nature'. I won't try to develop this theme directly, but merely say that my own recourse to the word 'spiritual' (and all important words are dangerous) is determined by the contemplation of a world in which the technologico-Bethamite ethos has triumphed at the expense of the human spirit—that is, of human life. There is an intrinsic human nature with needs that don't exist for the technologist and the Bethamite as such; there is a need for significance, for that which makes life significant—something that can't be discussed or taken account of in terms of what can be measured or averaged or defined, though rationality and intelligence (whether they know it or not) are thwarted when it fails.

Cry what shall I cry?
All flesh is grass: comprehending
The Companions of the Bath, the Knights of the British
    Empire, the Cavaliers
O Cavaliers! of the Legion of Honour,
The Order of the Black Eagle (1st and 2nd class),
And the Order of the Rising Sun.
Cry cry what shall I cry?

51

The first thing to do is to form the committees:
The consultative councils, the standing committees, select com-
mittees and sub-committees.
One secretary will do for several committees.
What shall I cry?

Whether or not in discussing that necessity of fully
human life which is wanting—discussing as Eliot evokes
it that which might meet human spiritual need—one
finds oneself dealing in Christian theology depends on
who one is. I myself think I am paying a high tribute to
the genius of the poet when I express my conviction that
as literary critic one had better not find oneself doing that
—and that it needs literary criticism to do justice to Eliot.

I endeavoured a good while ago to explain and enforce
that conviction in examining what was then extant of
Four Quartets, the occasion being the appearance of 'The
Dry Salvages', the third. These lines come towards the
end of it:

The hint half guessed, the gift half understood, is Incarnation.
Here the impossible union
Of spheres of existence is actual,
Here the past and future
Are conquered, and reconciled,
Where action were otherwise movement
Of that which is only moved
And has in it no source of movement . . .

How far the word 'Incarnation' has an effect of
charged potency, and how far, as summarizing the communication of the preceding poetry, it remains not much
more than an abstract word, will vary, I said, from
reader to reader; but there is no sleight, nothing but
openness, in the way the word presents itself at this point

in the poem as if drawn up into a gap, a crucial emptiness, which it rises inevitably to fill. Justice to Eliot, I insisted, entails the recognition that nothing of what Harding calls the 'cheapness' of *The Cocktail Party* is to be found in the poetry; there the attribution of 'heroic sincerity' gets its steady justification.

It still remains true that that disability is basic in Eliot which Harding notes in these terms (calling it a 'psychological over-simplification in the central argument of the play'):

> Eliot offers the view that only a small number of chosen or doomed people, the Saints, like Celia, can take the course that leads towards self-less love, in the sense of love for something fully outside themselves. Apart from these few saints, everyone is relegated to the condition of the Chamberlaynes and the possibility of a deeply satisfying human love is excluded without argument.

As I have already said, I can only see the disability manifested here as having serious consequences for his spiritual quest—having some of the effects of starvation on the nature of his spirituality. But we have to recognize, I think, that one of those effects was intensity, and without the intensity ... —I won't develop that consideration further than to say that the distinctive Eliotic intensity was a necessary condition of that astonishing feat of sustained creative integrity, *Four Quartets*.

That work I obviously can't offer to examine now. The whole hour wouldn't have been enough. My aim in any case was not completeness and self-contained justice. I have assumed in my audience a familiarity with Eliot's poetry, and my aim has been to convey as well as I could in an hour my sense of the form and distinctive nature of his achievement, now that we have it before us in its totality. I aimed at laying a given kind of emphasis—an emphasis that makes *Four Quartets* the culminating manifestation of Eliot's genius—the consummation of his creative career. The mere statement of that conviction (led up to by the general tenor of my argument) is what I must leave you with—except that, from a close examination I once made[1] of the first three parts of the whole work I will repeat this brief passage:

> That the poetry seems to invite a given intellectual and doctrinal frame may be found to recommend it. But the frame is another thing (and the prose is not the poetry—Eliot himself has made some relevant observations). The genius, that of a great poet, manifests itself in a profound and acute apprehension of the difficulties of his age. Those difficulties are such that they certainly cannot be met by any simple re-imposition of traditional frames. Eliot is known as professing Anglo-Catholicism and classicism; but his poetry is remarkable for the extraordinary resource, penetration and stamina with which it makes its explorations into the concrete actualities of experience below the conceptual currency; into the life that must be the *raison d'être* of any frame—while there's life at all. With all its positive aspiration and movement, it is at the same time essentially a work of radical analysis and revision, endlessly insistent in its care not to confuse the frame with the living reality, and heroic in its refusal to accept. In any case, to feel an immense indebtedness to Eliot and to recognize the immense indebtedness of the age, one doesn't need to share his intellectually formulated conclusions, his doctrinal views, or even to be uncritical of the attitudes of the poetry.

I haven't done Eliot justice. I haven't called attention to the extraordinary variety of his poetic manners, all so intensely Eliotic. This diversity in perfection is the more striking in that he was not a copious producer—indeed, those of us whose adult lives were contemporaneous with

---

[1] Reprinted as Appendix I in *Education and the University*.

his creative career felt he was decidedly otherwise. But the not massive total product we now have gives no effect of slightness. The constituent things are in their concentration so completely what they are, the development is so unforeseeable and yet so compelling in its logic, that the whole body of the poetry, as I've suggested already, affects us as one astonishing major work.

3
Yeats:
The Problem and the Challenge

YEATS:
THE PROBLEM AND THE
CHALLENGE

YEATS, for all his conviction of an essential affinity, was radically unlike Blake. I have marked a score or two of places in the collected poems where that comment has occurred to me. I start with it because it is certainly something that needs to be said, and because in an attempt to define Yeats's poetic character it must be a key emphasis. Not that I am going to develop it, or shall treat the theme systematically in any part of this lecture. Having introduced it in this way I shall be able to pick it up from time to time and it will be all the while implicitly present; at least, I mean it to be.

An undertaking of the kind to which I am committed has its own necessities of approach and procedure. I am committed, I had been inclined to say, to some rashness; but 'rashness' suggests irresponsibility, so I withdraw the word. What I must aim at is a quintessential economy, and it demands that I should be peculiarly responsible. The invitation I accepted to give this lecture came to me as a challenge, and I accepted it, not merely because of the flattering terms in which it was framed, but because I had already myself issued the challenge. I had told myself more than once that all those years (now a third of a century) having passed since, in the earliest beginnings of the recognition of Yeats as a major twentieth-century poet, I had with some care expressed my sense of what he had achieved and where he stood, I ought, now that his work had been long completed, and my notes and hieroglyphs had thickened in the margins, to attempt a *compte rendu*—something both bold and precise —once again. The precision aimed at entails economy, and the economy entails hazards—or, at any rate, in a world where there are many Yeats specialists (a portentous change since I first wrote on Yeats) one will necessarily seem to be 'asking for it'. There must be bold judgments, but they will have to rest on a minimal and highly selective presentation of the grounds.

We *have* now all the *œuvre*. That itself affects one's sense of Yeats—for there are significant developments. I have re-read him a good deal in recent years; I have discussed him this past academic year with keen and well-read undergraduates at my new university; and I have gone through and pondered the whole body of poems. My sense of Yeats and of his place in English literature hasn't changed much. But I now lay more emphasis on the question: How much of the fully achieved thing *is* there in Yeats's *œuvre*—what proportion of the wholly created poem that stands there unequivocally in its own right, self-sufficient? I have in mind the period of his work in which he challenges us to think of him as a major poet. And it seems to me that the proportion is not large.

And there is the problem I had in view in my title. It is a problem of critical statement that is (which is why it matters) one of critical *compte rendu*—the problem of arriving at a clear critical recognition of just what Yeats's achievement was. For confusion is very possible, and confusion is a bad thing. It tends, I think, to prevail— which is bad (shall I say) for the causes to which Yeats devoted his life. To have started as a belated Victorian Romantic poet, to have won a distinctive place as such, and then to have developed a poetic as decidedly twentieth-century and post-Edwardian as Eliot's—that is a great achievement. Expression is only altered by a man of genius—Eliot's own dictum, as you know: Yeats too had genius. To describe the alteration he effected isn't a simple matter, and to say this is a compliment. The poetic he created for himself has considerable variety, range and flexibility. In touch with the spoken living language and the speaking voice, it admits of many tones and the expression of complex and subtly changing attitudes. There is no element of a man's experience in the twentieth-century that, of its nature, it excludes.

Yet one couldn't in 1919, when I began to read seriously in contemporary literature, have attributed any such achievement to Yeats, who had then been writing through three full decades, and was forming the habit of presenting himself in his verse (an un-Blakelike characteristic) as an aging man. He had already been going a long while, and was an established name, when I first began reading poetry as a boy—say seven or eight years before the war. The poems by which he was known were congenial to the late Victorian taste of that Edwardian-Georgian period, and, in spite of the suggestion of ancient and obscure Irishness, presented no difficulty. In their hypnoidal vaguenesses ('dim', 'dream-pale') and incantory rhythms they exemplify that preoccupation with creating a dream-world, or poetic otherworld, which Eliot in a famous essay noted as a characteristic of Victorian poetry.

In 1919, from when my continuous cultivated interest in modern poetry dates, I read *The Wild Swans At Coole*, and I read Middleton Murry's review of it in the *Athenaeum*. I thought it, and still think it, a very good review (it is to be found in *Aspects of Literature*). It is entitled 'Mr Yeats's Swan Song' and in it Murry says: 'He remains an artist by determination, even though he returns downcast and depressed from the great quest of poetry', and 'His sojourn in the world of the imagination, far from enriching his vision, has made it infinitely tenuous'. Contemplating such poems as 'I am worn out with dreams' and 'The Collar-bone of a Hare', Murry says 'Not even the regret is passionate; it is pitiful. . . . It is pitiful because, even now in spite of all his honesty, the poet mistakes the cause of his sorrow. He is worn out not with dreams, but with the vain effort to master them and submit them to his own creative energy. He has not subdued them nor built a new world for them; he has merely followed them like will-o-the-wisps away from the world he knows. Now, possessing neither world, he sits by the edge of a barren road that vanishes into a no-man's-land, where there is no future, and whence there is no way back to the past.' Murry doesn't say anything about developments, in the collections leading up to this latest, towards a new art of poetic expression, post-Victorian and post-nineties, but who at that date would, or could, have done? For who could then have seen in Yeats the potentiality of a major poet?

It was *The Tower*, coming—most remarkable fact—when Yeats was over sixty that made the difference. The hindsight then became possible with the advantage of which one saw point—in fact, a decided critical interest—in tracing the development of Yeats's poetic from *The Wind Among the Reeds* onwards; for one saw that there had been a development into such command of expression as implied, for consummation and *raison d'être*, a modern major poetry. It isn't essential for my inevitably limited purpose to attempt the tracing. That purpose entails an insistence, very necessary (may I be allowed to say?) now that the study of Yeats as a major poet has become an academic institution, on the firm and clear recognition without which such an inquiry can't be undertaken intelligently, and with critical profit.

It is important to insist, then, that Yeats's great poems aren't many. It doesn't follow that only they are worth having. But the interest of the total *œuvre*, an intelligent appreciation of the significance and genuine value, depends on one's being clear about the restrictive effect of the most essential kind of evaluative judgment. Yeats's great poems are a very small proportion of the whole. It is an immediately relevant point—and I speak with the emphasis of personal experience when I say this—that it was the appearance of *The Tower* in 1928 that made it possible to think of claiming for Yeats the status of a modern poet who demanded to be considered along with Eliot.

I remember vividly the impact of *The Tower*, of which I have a first edition, acquired in the way in which I have acquired such first editions as I have had—I bought it when it came out. There, at the very beginning of the book, was one of Yeats's major successes; there was one of his great poems—the first that one was to know: 'Sailing to Byzantium'. I see that, troubled as I am by the problem of economy, I must give this poem some particular attention. The troubling force of the problem immediately is that I know I can't find time to read out the uninterrupted whole either first or finally, but must confine myself to reading the poem in bits, with breaks for commentary. But I can assume that, as an organically knit whole, it is familiar enough to prevail against the disruptive process. Before starting I will make some general observations that would not have been preliminary if there had been time for me to read the poem out first.

The distinctively post-Victorian kind of organic complexity that Yeats has here achieved is suggested when one says that 'Sailing to Byzantium' lends itself as little to paraphrase as Eliot's almost contemporary 'Marina' does. If one tries to render the sense in prose one finds very soon that one is committed to exegesis and the description of an organization that is utterly unproselike. The impulsions and interests out of which the poem comes are those which we know as the inveterate Yeatsian themes—these form the thematic material (for, in emphasizing the essentially unproselike mode—which nevertheless demands the full waking attention of the thinking mind, one can't help invoking the musical analogy).

There are, given an added poignancy by the nostalgia for lost youth, the compelling values represented by the words 'love' and 'life'; there is the recoil from transience and age; and there is the preoccupation with the eternal— an escape from transience and an assurance of a real reality that shall transcend time. The poem is an organic structure of the motions, the impulsions, the recoils and contradictions and incompatibles, suggested by that account. The contradictions and incompatibles are reconciled only in that they make a compelling, or convincing poem; problems are evoked with intensity, but there is no solution. The poem is convincing; it satisfies as a tense and vital totality. Nothing could be less like Johnson's conception of an acceptable poem—or, to take a distinguished and sophisticated mind of a nearer age (I as an editor had the honour of printing him once) George Santayana's. For them the poet should know

beforehand what his thought is to be and what his conclusions. But Yeats in such a poem as 'Sailing to
Byzantium' discovers, or determines (for 'discover' suggests a kind of conscious recognition there may never
have been), where he stands in relation to thought, conclusion and belief as he composes—in the composing:
the process of composition, a matter of much piecing,
patching and redrafting, is the process of discovery or
determination.

And this is the moment at which to say that too often
Yeats, working at a poem, lets his extra-poetic habits get
in the way of poetic success. 'Poetic success' here means
a kind of convincingness and inevitability that comes of,
that *is*, a complete sincerity—the sincerity that is of the
whole being, and not merely a matter of conscious intention. To explain what I mean by 'extra-poetic' habits I
need only point to *A Vision*, that representative of a lifelong quasi-creative addiction which was not sharply or
surely distinguished by Yeats from his real creative
concern. That Yeats had this addiction, and the addic-
tions to the occult and the esoteric that went with it, is
an important datum; the evidence is there in various ways
in his poetry. And I am not saying anything so simple as
that they are all to be regretted and wished away. But I
do say that there is no good reason for supposing that
one need study the schematisms, the diagrammatics, the
symbolical elaborations to which Yeats devoted so much
of his energy. At a time when the professional study of
literature has grown so portentously there is point in
putting aside the refinements and qualifications possible
in a fuller statement and insisting, with emphasis, that a
close critical appreciation of a successful poem of Yeats
doesn't require that one should bring up any special

knowledge or instructions from outside. One can invoke
Coleridge's well-known dictum, to the effect that a poem
should contain within itself the reason why it is so and
not otherwise. To suppose that Yeats is a special case to
which this doesn't apply is a mischievous delusion—a
point to which I shall revert.

I will now read the opening stanza of 'Sailing to
Byzantium':

> *That is no country for old men. The young*
> *In one another's arms, birds in the trees,*
> *—Those dying generations—at their song,*
> *The salmon-falls, the mackerel-crowded seas,*
> *Fish, flesh, or fowl, commend all summer long*
> *Whatever is begotten born and dies.*
> *Caught in that sensual music all neglect*
> *Monuments of unaging intellect.*

The poet is so clearly drawn to what in that stanza he
evokes with such force and poignancy that when one
comes to the 'Monuments of unaging intellect' one can't
help taking them with an ironical effect of *pis-aller*. And
a sardonic irony will indeed be found to have had a
determining part in the total effect of the poem. Nevertheless the second stanza makes it plain that the concern
for the eternal has not, after all, been summarily 'placed':

> *An aged man is but a paltry thing,*
> *A tattered coat upon a stick, unless*
> *Soul clap its hands and sing, and louder sing,*
> *For every tatter in its mortal dress,*
> *Nor is there singing school but studying*
> *Monuments of its own magnificence;*
> *And therefore I have sailed the seas and come*
> *To the holy city of Byzantium.*

The very frankness of the opening—'An aged man is but a paltry thing ... *unless*'—serves to emphasize the positiveness of the belief, or emotional investment, represented by 'monuments' while this mood prevails. The stanza, as one can't but illustrate in reading it out, moves forward with a lift the significance of which is unmistakable. The 'singing' of 'singing school' invests the 'studying', paradoxically, with the evoked gladness and life-affirmation of the first stanza, so associating the 'monuments' with a suggested higher life that shall transcend the disadvantages fated to the generations of 'whatever is begotten born and dies'. 'Byzantium', a symbol both pregnant and indeterminate, has for its clear immediate function to suggest the antithesis of the world of nature—the world of 'those dying generations'. Why the poet should have found the indeterminateness congenial to his need comes out in the next stanza:

> *O sages standing in God's holy fire*
> *As in the gold mosaic of a wall,*
> *Come from the holy fire, perne in a gyre,*
> *And be the singing masters of my soul.*
> *Consume my heart away; sick with desire*
> *And fastened to a dying animal*
> *It knows not what it is; and gather me*
> *Into the artifice of eternity.*

We know by now that, whatever the total effect of the poem may turn out to be, it will hardly be affirmation. The poet's heart 'knows not what it is' nor what it wants, and the theme (if that is the word) or burden of the poem is the given kind of poignant, and humanly representative, indeterminateness. Intensely the soul interrogates itself and its images of fulfilment and finds no answer that doesn't turn into an irony.

67

> *. . . sick with desire*
> *And fastened to a dying animal*

—the ambiguity is essential and undeniable: Which is it—nostalgia for that country which is not for old men, or nostalgia for the eternal posited as the antithesis? The poet couldn't, I think, have said, and in any case the question isn't his but ours. The poem gives us the ambiguity; and then, we note, the invocation of the sages completes itself and the stanza with the appeal to

> *. . . gather me*
> *Into the artifice of eternity,*

about which the important thing to say is, not that it's a resolution, but that it's the ambiguity turning into an irony. The ironical force of 'artifice' is developed in the last stanza. It is a felicity of surprise that illustrates well the 'metaphysical' suppleness of Yeats's mature poetic art:

> *Once out of nature I shall never take*
> *My bodily form from any natural thing,*
> *But such a form as Grecian goldsmiths make*
> *Of hammered gold and gold enamelling*
> *To keep a drowsy emperor awake;*
> *Or set upon a golden bough to sing*
> *To lords and ladies of Byzantium*
> *Of what is past, or passing, or to come.*

The 'monuments of unaging intellect' with all the impressive associations of Byzantium—esoteric wisdom, metaphysico-theosophical cult and mystery, hieratic art —have been reduced to a clockwork toy, and the song of this now (after the promise of the 'singing school' in stanza III) represents the higher life or reality that was

to compensate for the lost song of those 'dying generations'. The duplicity of the last line gives the completing
touch to the irony:

> *Of what is past, or passing, or to come.*

This retains, inevitably, something of the solemn vatic
suggestion that emanates from the foregoing poem. But
what in its immediate context of the closing half-stanza
it evokes is court-gossip.

I am not saying that the irony is the irony of one who
passes an ironical verdict and mocks (that stage comes
later in Yeats). It is the irony of a tormenting complexity
of experience—a complexity that entails an irreducible
and tormenting contradiction of impulsions or imperatives
or verdicts. In the poem Yeats attains a tense and tentative poise, but, as is intimated by the irony (unforeseen
when he started, we have reason from the drafts for
guessing) in which the poem does nevertheless in a
natural way come to rest, this is no index of an achieved
stability. I open here what should be a major critical
theme for the student of Yeats, but obviously I can't do
much by way of developing it.

Something I can with economy do is to look comparatively at 'Byzantium', the closely related poem from *The
Winding Stair*. I shall at the same time be able to enforce
and carry further another point I have already made:
'Sailing to Byzantium' is (as a poem *should* be) self-
sufficient; it doesn't demand for its appreciation that one
should bring up from outside any knowledge of special
intentions on Yeats's part, or of the elaborate systems
that form their context. When I first read the poem the
New English Dictionary didn't help me with 'perne'
('perne in a gyre'), but I wasn't seriously troubled; the

poetic context charged the word sufficiently for its function. Now that I *know* what 'perne' literally means the
poem has gained nothing. On the contrary, not only
would the pre-Yeatsian meaning be a nuisance in itself
if thought of; the loaded 'perne' added to 'gyre' makes
it more difficult for the reader to repress the movement
of irritation aroused in him by the Yeatsian technicality
of the phrase, which stands out from the poem, and
proposes another context. But the major temptation to
the exegete is 'Byzantium', though that symbol pretty
obviously needs no commentary, since, for any educated
person who can read poetry, it works without help as the
poem requires. I say 'obviously', but the point I have to
make is that the habit of specialist exegesis doesn't favour
the recognition of a truth of that kind, critically important
as it is.

This may be illustrated by the way in which the poem
'Byzantium' from *The Winding Stair* is commonly
exalted above 'Sailing to Byzantium'—that, at least, is
the impression I have brought away from the books on
Yeats I have read. The accepted view, I gather, is that
'Byzantium', the later poem, is the 'richer'—I have seen
that word used of it by more than one Yeatsian. It is a
view that only the habit of the Yeats specialist can
explain—the habit of taking the opportunities offered by
the text to invoke Yeats's prose-elaborations and bring
into the poem what isn't there, and what one wouldn't
take to be there if one were 'trusting' the poem (I invoke
Lawrence). Respect for Yeats's genius dictates that one
should if possible read his poems as poems. And if one
reads 'Byzantium' as a poem one sees that the total
attitude is, beyond question, comparatively simple.

One might very well say bluntly of this poem that its

mood is sardonic bitterness. On the one hand, what is so irresistibly given in the opening stanza of 'Sailing to Byzantium'—'the young in one another's arms', the sensual music—is virtually absent, and, on the other, where the eternal is concerned, there is no suggestion of soul's clapping its hands and singing. I will again read stanza by stanza, making the minimal commentary. Instead of the opening stanza I have just recalled we now have this:

> *The unpurged images of day recede;*
> *The Emperor's drunken soldiery are abed;*
> *Night resonance recedes, night-walkers' song*
> *After great cathedral gong;*
> *A starlit or a moonlit dome disdains*
> *All that man is,*
> *All mere complexities,*
> *The fury and the mire of human veins.*

The tone is given in that dominating rime-word, 'disdains', which entails the following emphasis on 'All'. Ostensibly it defines the relation as now conceived or felt between 'all that man is' and the eternal. And all that man is reduces to

> *mere complexities,*
> *The fury and the mire of human veins.*

The disdain goes with the bitterness that is a strong element in the poem. The one like the other is, in whatever way conveyed, Yeats's, and they relate to the other un-Blakean characteristic, the pride that figures so much in the attitudes of Yeats's poetry.

This poem no more than 'Sailing to Byzantium' starts with a given foreseen balance of tones and stresses, a calculated total economy, in view. Its organization has nothing of the expository about it, and is not to be explained by reference to any supposed Yeatsian scheme in the background. It has the livingness of enacted self-discovery, brought by the technical skill of the poet to the satisfyingness of a completed poem—analogically a musical satisfyingness, and for us an index of sincerity. Yeats's poetic mastery appears in the delicate shifts of distance, tone and attack. So at the second stanza we have the change to the hushed, intent and personal; we are with Yeats at a séance, some experiment in magic and the occult, an invocation of the dead. Given in dramatic immediacy, there is the questioning of ontological status that greets, and takes stock of, the apparition:

> *Before me floats an image, man or shade,*
> *Shade more than man, more image than a shade;*
> *For Hades' bobbin bound in mummy-cloth*
> *May unwind the winding path;*
> *A mouth that has no moisture and no breath*
> *Breathless mouths may summon . . .*

Then, from the note of generalizing consideration into which the questioning has passed, the poet, as if arrived at a sudden resolution of doubt, breaks into action—for the effect on us is that:

> *I hail the superhuman;*
> *I call it death-in-life and life-in-death.*

Which is it? There is surely a difference. To 'hail the superhuman' as 'death-in-life' *and* 'life-in-death' with that air of ecstatic assurance is to transcend the balancing of doubt and belief in irony; to drop thought in an act, the act being an expression of intense sardonic bitterness.

This prevails through the rest of the poem. It is attributed in the next stanza, paralogically but the more significantly, to the golden toy, whose mechanical singing it is that now replaces that of the 'dying generations'. In a quasi-musical way the opening of the stanza echoes, with an effect of pointless ironic dryness, the ontological opening of the previous stanza:

> *Miracle, bird or golden handiwork,*
> *More miracle than bird or handiwork,*
> *Planted on the starlit golden bough,*
> *Can like the cocks of Hades crow,*
> *Or, by the moon embittered, scorn aloud*
> *In glory of changeless metal*
> *Common bird or petal*
> *And all complexities of mire or blood.*

The great temptation to fully equipped commentators comes with the next stanza. But we don't at all need the help they bring from Yeats's reading about Byzantium. In fact, in my own observation it serves only to distract the commentator from the actuality of Yeats's poetry, which is here not obscure. It doesn't matter from what reading, what tradition about spirits, purgation and the Emperor's pavement the memory came; the poetry that came of the memory is self-sufficient, and its significance clear. The 'flames that no faggot feeds' are the 'holy fire' from which the sages of the earlier poem are bidden to come and 'be the singing masters of my soul'. 'Flames begotten of flame', independent of matter, they represent a purely spiritual potency. The spirits *suffering* purgation are 'blood-begotten'—it is that body-soul antithesis which Yeats (unlike Blake in this too) finds so troubling. What, in the face of the exegetical habit, needs to be emphasized if one is concerned with poetic significance, is the evoked sense of agonized futility in which the stanza ends. This is what, in this self-imposed ordeal of self-questioning and

F

self-realization (a major poem for Yeats *was* that), the hope of escaping from time and the complexities of mire and blood has become for him.

I have anticipated with my own comments in this way in order that I may go on to read the rest of the poem—two stanzas—to the close:

> *At midnight on the Emperor's pavement flit*
> *Flames that no faggot feeds, nor steel has lit,*
> *Nor storm disturbs, flames begotten of flame,*
> *Where blood-begotten spirits come*
> *And all complexities of fury leave,*
> *Dying into a dance,*
> *An agony of trance,*
> *An agony of flame that cannot singe a sleeve.*
>
> *Astraddle on the dolphin's mire and blood,*
> *Spirit after spirit! The smithies break the flood,*
> *The golden smithies of the Emperor!*
> *Marbles of the dancing floor*
> *Break bitter furies of complexity,*
> *Those images that yet*
> *Fresh images beget,*
> *That dolphin-torn, that gong-tormented sea.*

The nature and significance of the bitterness come out in the offer to reduce the 'dolphin' itself to mire and blood —for the traditional association of the dolphin, friend of man, with a vitality and a grace that are at the same time both physical and more than that is strong enough to insist on itself decisively here: there is a discord.

The two 'Byzantium' poems, in their likeness and their difference, associate very closely and form together an impressive achievement. The quasi-musical way in which they treat their thematic material, organize their complexities of impulse and attitude, and bring together their tensions, contradictions and irreconcilables into satisfying totalities makes them triumphs of a wholly original art of creative expression that is contemporary with Eliot's. The originality is of the order that we know as the mark of genius; they are major poetry. Yet they stand apart; I know of no other successes of that kind in the collected volume of Yeats.

Why this should be so isn't hard to understand. 'Sailing to Byzantium' doesn't come out of any wholeness of being or mastery of experience; its poetic or quasi-musical satisfyingness as a totality is not an index of any permanent stability achieved by the poet in life. The contradictions, uncertainties and shifting stresses that, exploratorily, wondering what he is ('sick with desire, he knows not what he is'), Yeats for once succeeds—astonishingly at sixty—in dealing with creatively, don't favour the repetition of that kind of success. The energy that achieved it has become in 'Byzantium' unmistakably the energy of desperation, intense with the 'bitter furies of complexity'. He is ready to hand over to Crazy Jane and Jack the Journeyman, who represent the abandonment of all concern for the resolution, or paradoxically creative management, of the complexity.

It is characteristic of Yeats to have had no centre of unity, and to have been unable to find one. The lack is apparent in his solemn propoundings about the Mask and the Anti-self, and in the related schematic elaborations. It is there, an essential theme for the critic, in that habit of cultivating attitudes and postures which makes one—if an Englishman, at any rate—remark that Yeats is a fellow-countryman of Wilde, Shaw and Joyce (I am thinking of that photograph of Joyce with his walking-stick outside Shakespeare and Co.). It is not a simple theme; that is why it presents an essential interest for the critic. We have something that is at least intimately associated with the habit in Yeats's attainment of a poetic that enables him to be both noble and distinctively twentieth-century. With the valid and impressive nobility of *tenue*—

> *Beauty like a tightend bow, a kind*
> *That is not natural in an age like this*

—go the devotion to the ideal beauty here personified in Maud Gonne, and the importance assigned to patrician 'civilization' as represented by Coole Park and Lady Gregory. We may think that the relative value-affirmations aren't, a mature scale of value and a mature experience being in question, altogether acceptable, but nevertheless we have to testify that in Yeats's poetry certain genuine validities are, with a poet's realizing force, presented creatively so as to be compelling in themselves. But with the nobility goes the habit of aspiring to

> *dine at journey's end*
> *With Landor and with Donne.*

He owes something to both poets, but with the addiction to Landor and the odd coupling go his talk about the *élite* of great Irishmen to which he belongs—Swift (an Englishman who hated Ireland), Berkeley, Burke, Goldsmith, Grattan—and his proud conviction that he had no blood of any huckster in his veins. Closely related, the significance being enforced by the 'Hard-riding country gentlemen' and the 'Porter-drinkers' randy laughter' that come in the same paragraph of 'Under Ben Bulben', is his choosing to close that valedictory poem (but for the epitaph and the brief prelude to it) with a self-gratulatory salute to the 'indomitable Irishry'. And the epitaph itself—

> *Cast a cold eye*
> *On life, on death.*
> *Horseman, pass by!*

—belongs, surely, to the category of attitudes that are struck.

Perhaps by now I have made it plain why, prompted by Yeats's own contrary suggestion, I started by saying that he is very unlike Blake. I don't myself believe that Blake had a comprehensive guiding wisdom to offer, but it was his genius to be capable of a complete disinterestedness, and therefore of a complete sincerity. He had a rare integrity, and a rare sense of responsibility as a focus of life. His experience was *his* because only in the individual focus can there *be* experience, but his concern to perceive and understand was undeflected by egotism, or by any impulse to protect an image of himself. He was not tempted to form one. 'Beauty like a tightened bow'— such a phrase couldn't have come from Blake, the artist and poet who speaks so characteristically of the 'wiry bounding line'. He couldn't have produced the portentous nonsense about 'number' that Yeats offers us in 'The Statues', that solemn parody of his esoterico-metaphysical vein. The 'wiry bounding line' is a living line, alive with the energy it conveys and defines, 'energy' in Blake's idiom being a spontaneous organic creativity that is the essence of life. His awareness of terrible complexities, and of problems for which he has no solutions, doesn't entail any protest against the essential conditions of life. The insistent emphasis on 'dying generations' and the obsessed raging against inevitable age—these for Blake were sicknesses to be diagnosed.

I have been leading up in these last remarks to a mention—it can, now, be only a mention, or little more—of the poem of Yeats's which I like more than any other: 'Among School Children'. Its relevance at this point is that it presents, and implicitly proposes, the criteria I have been invoking in my comparative references to Blake. The characteristic Yeatsian themes are there, but the prevailing tone and the total attitude are different; the sardonic bitterness and the Swiftian note are absent—there is no hint of them. There is indeed a faint wryness about the touch of dramatized self with which the opening stanza closes; he sees himself for a moment through the children's eyes, which

> *In momentary wonder stare upon*
> *A sixty-year-old smiling public man.*

But the note is one of matter-of-fact acceptance, and Yeats clearly takes a natural satisfaction in his public standing as Senator Yeats. The 'I dream' with which the next stanza begins—

> *I dream of a Ledaean body, bent*
> *Above a sinking fire, a tale that she*
> *Told of a harsh reproof, or trivial event*
> *That changed some childish day to tragedy—*
> *Told, and it seemed that our two natures blent*
> *Into a sphere from youthful sympathy*

—introduces a retrospective survey, or audit, of a life's main preoccupations, which is developed as if it were in reverie. But the conclusion has a force of convinced and irresistible truth, coming as it does with (to use the analogy again) a perfect cogency of musical logic:

78

O Presences
That passion, piety or affection knows,
And that all heavenly glory symbolise—
O self-born mockers of man's enterprise;

Labour is blossoming or dancing where
The body is not bruised to pleasure soul,
Nor beauty born out of its own despair,
Nor blear-eyed wisdom out of midnight oil.
O chestnut-tree, great-rooted blossomer,
Are you the leaf, the blossom or the bole?
O body swayed to music, O brightening glance,
How can we know the dancer from the dance?

There is nothing else like that in the collected poems. So far from its being the proof of an achieved stability and wholeness in the poet, the ugliest and most disturbing expressions of inner discord and rebellion or despair to be found in his *œuvre* mark his final phase. And about the significance of Crazy Jane and her accompaniments I will say no more; it is surely plain.

What I must do in closing is to revert to the question of where, in sum, Yeats stands among the poets—or, more generally, of what place he holds in English literature. The volume containing 'Sailing to Byzantium' and 'Among School Children' impressed one—and impresses —as coming from a major poet. And yet even that volume is disappointing; for how much in it can be placed with those two poems? I know of persons of judgment who think highly of 'Leda and the Swan', but it seems to me to have too much of Parnassian art about it to be thought of as coming from the great original poet who 'altered expression'. I mention it because, in the range of Yeats's art, it represents something of a foil to the very characteristic mode we have in the reverie-poems: I am thinking of the title-poem, 'The Tower', 'Meditations in Time of Civil War', 'Nineteen Hundred and Nineteen', and 'All Souls' Night'. And what I want to say about *them* is that though they represent in diction and manner a creative habit without which we shouldn't have had the great poems and though, with the body of verse that associates with them in technical ethos, they count immensely in our sense of Yeats as a major poet, they are not themselves among the great poems. They aren't closely enough organized and they haven't, as wholes, an intense enough life.

This is neither doing them critical justice nor suggesting their interest. Still less is it possible to illustrate representatively the kinds of interest that make the collected volume a book to read through from time to time. The point I've been wanting to make can be put in a comparative way; the sense one has of Yeats's major status is differently constituted from that which one has of Eliot's. Where Eliot is in question it is the economy, concentration, perfected art and assured creative purpose of the body of achieved poetry that tells. 'Perfected' is perhaps not altogether the right word for *The Waste Land*; but *The Waste Land* leads on to the succession of poems in the different perfected modes—from *Ash-Wednesday* to *Four Quartets*—that seems, in its unpredictable but consistent development, like one quintessential poetic work. And that, for us, *is* Eliot. But where Yeats is in question, while it is because of the poet that we are concerned with the man and the life, we *are* concerned with them—inescapably. The most resolutely literary-critical study of his poetic career entails biography, personalities, public affairs and history.

Yeats's status as a major figure in English literature is

bound up with that truth, and to insist that a poem is to be judged as a poem and that literary criticism is a discipline for an exacting kind of relevance in response and comment is not to contradict it. You can't discuss the development by which Yeats finally achieved the poetic of 'Sailing to Byzantium' and 'Among School Children' without going into a great part of the literary history of half a century, and, as you ponder the amount of reference that that involves both to Yeats's personal life and to the civilization he lived in, you will find yourself once again asking (it is a salutary exercise): 'But what *is* literary history?' That is not, of course, asked to be answered. The point regards the way in which Yeats's career poses the insistent questions of the place, part and possibility of the major artist in modern civilization.

4
A Fresh Approach to 'Wuthering Heights'

PREFATORY NOTE

I took to Adams House, Harvard and to Cornell in 1966 a mass of material on and about *Wuthering Heights*, some of it written out in full for lecturing and some in note form for seminars and for the discussions that I hoped would arise out of the lectures, of which I delivered one at Adam's House, Harvard, and one at Cornell. These two lectures were made out of various parts of my material with a good deal of overlapping; but there remained much that was unused, even in conversation, which I had been using in working with Cambridge undergraduates in England for some years. When the lectures—inseparable Siamese twins—were to be written out for publication, it was necessary to include all I had taken, in order to make my case out convincingly, as well as in order to satisfy my purpose, which was, to put into circulation grounds for a responsible and sensitive approach to *Wuthering Heights* in its context (both literary and historical) as well as to provide a fresh assessment, which should also be corrective, of its merits absolutely as a literary creation. Where my material fell outside the direct line of my argument, I have relegated it to appendices, but since the conclusions drawn therefrom are necessary to enforce my case, I hope the appendices will be read as part of the whole.

Q. D. L.

A FRESH APPROACH TO
'WUTHERING HEIGHTS'

AFTER its initial adverse reception ('too odiously and abominably pagan to be palatable to the most vitiated class of English readers'—*The Quarterly Review*) and its subsequent installation as a major English classic (of such mystic significance that while its meaning transcends criticism adverse comment on any concrete features would be in the worst taste), *Wuthering Heights*, to my knowledge as a university teacher of English literature, seems to be coming under attack from a new generation. To those who find the novel mainly melodrama, complain that the violence is factitious or sadistic, or object (with justice) to the style as often stilted and uneven, and to those who can see no coherent intention but find incompatible fragments and disjointed intentions at different levels of seriousness, an answer that the novel's greatness is unquestionable is useless. Some of these charges cannot be altogether refuted, though they can be generally accounted for as inevitable features of the kind of undertaking by such a writer at such a date, and some agreement reached about the nature of the success of the book on the whole: for that *Wuthering Heights* is a striking achievement of some kind candid readers can and do feel. The difficulty of establishing that a literary work is a classic is nothing compared to the difficulty of establishing *what kind* of a classic it is—what is in fact the nature of its success, what kind of creation it represents. One has only to read the admiring critics of *Wuthering Heights*, even more the others, to see that there is no agreed reading of this novel at all. Desperate attempts to report a flawless work of art lead to a dishonest ignoring of recalcitrant elements or an interpretation of them which is sophistical; other and more sustained sophistry has resulted from such academic bright ideas as the one confidently asserted to me in an American university by a professor of English Literature who had discovered that 'The clue to *Wuthering Heights* is that Nelly Dean is Evil'.

Of course, in general one attempts to achieve a reading of a text which includes all its elements, but here I believe we must be satisfied with being able to account for some of them and concentrate on what remains. It is better to admit that some of the difficulties of grasping what is truly creative in *Wuthering Heights* are due to the other parts—to the author in her inexperience having made false starts, changing her mind (as tone and style suggest) probably because of rewriting from earlier stories with themes she had lost interest in and which have become submerged, though not assimilated, in the final work.[1] Another source of confusion to the reader is that she tried to do too much, too many different things (a common trouble in first novels and in most Victorian novels)

[1] Mr Justice Vaisey, giving a legal opinion on the text ('The Authorship of *Wuthering Heights*', Brontë Society Publications, 1946), notes such a distinction in 'diction, style and taste' between 'the introductory portion' and the rest of the book, that he believed it to indicate two authors; which would give ground to an old theory or tradition that Emily worked from a manuscript of Branwell's at the start (joint composition being probably a practice of the Brontë children, and Emily and Patrick are said to have written practically indistinguishable minute hands). Writing at two different periods by Emily alone, and at the earlier under the influence of Branwell or in deliberate imitation of his style (as Lockwood) would, however, account for such a disparity.

and that some of these interfere with her deeper intentions—though of course this is also one source of the richness of this novel and we wouldn't care to sacrifice many of these, I think. The novel has all the signs of having been written at different times (because in different styles) and with varying intentions; we must sort these out in order to decide what *is* the novel. In spite of the brilliantly successful time-shifts and what has been called, not very happily, the 'Chinese box' ingenuity of construction, it certainly isn't a seamless 'work of art', and candour obliges us to admit ultimately that some things in the novel are incompatible with the rest, so much so that one seems at times to find oneself in really different novels.

Even criticism that is felt to be very helpful because unusually honest and sensitive may end by leaving the stress in the wrong place. I will instance a pioneer critique, Mr Klingopulos's revaluation of *Wuthering Heights* in *Scrutiny* under our collaborative heading 'The Novel as Dramatic Poem'. In 1947, when we published it, it was very salutary that *Wuthering Heights* should thus be rescued from the woolly treatment that was then current (e.g., in Lord David Cecil's *Early Victorian Novelists*). But in order to make the case and points he felt needed making, Mr Klingopulos ignores or slights elements and scenes which impinge on me, at least, as of fundamental importance. For instance, though he starts by saying, very properly, that 'the main problems in any account of the book are these: to decide on the status of Catherine and her relationship with Edgar and Heathcliff: to decide on the status of the Cathy–Hareton relationship and the appropriateness of reading it as a comment on what happened earlier',—nothing could be better than this clearing of the ground—yet he makes Catherine as a matter of course the splendid and valuable creature of conventional esteem (without noting Nelly's, Edgar's and at times Heathcliff's 'placing' of her, as well as more subtle insights of the novelist's own), and he goes so far as to assert as a general truth of *Wuthering Heights* that 'the author's preferences are not shown' and therefore, he deduces, it is not 'a moral tale'. Actually, I shall argue, the author's preferences *are* shown, Catherine is judged by the author in the parallel but notably different history of the daughter who, inheriting her mother's name, and likenesses both physical and psychological, is shown by deliberate choice, and trial and error, developing the maturity and therefore achieving the happiness, that the mother failed in, whereas we have seen the mother hardening into a fatal immaturity which destroys herself and those (Heathcliff and Edgar principally) involved with her. Nor is the author's impersonality (deliberately maintained by the device of a narrator who records other narrators and all of whom are much less like their creator than Conrad's Marlow his)—nor is that impersonality inconsistent with a moral intention. That is, the reader is obliged to draw moral conclusions, from the very nature of the scenes and actors in whose lives he is involved by sympathy and compassion or horror and repulsion.

I would first like to clear out of the way the *confusions* of the plot and note the different levels on which the novel operates at different times. It seems clear to me that Emily Brontë had some trouble in getting free of a false start—a start which suggests that we are going to have a regional version of the sub-plot of *Lear* (Shakespeare being generally the inspiration for those early nineteenth-century novelists who rejected the eighteenth-century idea of the novel). In fact, the Lear-world of violence, cruelty, unnatural crimes, family disruption and physical horrors remains the world of the household at Wuthering Heights, a characteristic due not to sadism or perversion in the novelist (some of the physical violence is quite unrealized)[1] but to the Shakespearian intention. The troubles of the Earnshaws started when the father brought home the boy Heathcliff (of which he gives an unconvincing explanation and for whom he shows an unaccountable weakness) and forced him on the protesting family; Heathcliff 'the cuckoo' by intrigue soon ousts the legitimate son Hindley and, like Edmund, Gloucester's natural son in *Lear*, his malice brings about the ruin of two families (the Earnshaws and the Lintons, his rival getting the name Edgar by attraction from *Lear*). Clearly, Heathcliff was originally the illegitimate son and Catherine's half-brother, which would explain why, though so attached to him by early associations and natural sympathies, Catherine never really thinks of him as a possible lover either before or after marriage;[2] it also explains why all the children slept in one bed at the Heights till adolescence, we gather (we learn later from Catherine (Chapter XII) that being removed at puberty from this bed became a turning-point in her inner life, and this is only one of the remarkable insights which *Wuthering Heights* adds to the Romantic poets' exploration of childhood experience). The favourite Romantic

[1] *v.* Appendix B.

[2] The speech (Chap. IX) in which Catherine explains to Nelly why she couldn't marry Heathcliff—on social grounds—belongs to the sociological *Wuthering Heights*. But even then she intends, she declares, to keep up her old (sisterly) relations with him, to help him get on in the world—'to *rise*' as she significantly puts it in purely social terms.

theme of incest therefore must have been the impulsion behind the earliest conception of *Wuthering Heights*. Rejecting this story for a more mature intention, Emily Brontë was left with hopeless inconsistencies on her hands, for while Catherine's feelings about Heathcliff are never sexual (though she feels the bond of sympathy with a brother to be more important to her than her feelings for her young husband), Heathcliff's feelings for her are always those of a lover. As Heathcliff has been written out as a half-brother, Catherine's innocent refusal to see that there is anything in her relation to him incompatible with her position as a wife, becomes preposterous and the impropriety which she refuses to recognize is translated into social terms—Edgar thinks the kitchen the suitable place for Heathcliff's reception by Mrs Linton while she insists on the parlour. Another trace of the immature draft of the novel is the fairy-tale opening of the Earnshaw story, where the father, like the merchant in *Beauty and the Beast*, goes off to the city promising to bring his children back the presents each has commanded: but the fiddle was smashed and the whip lost so the only present he brings for them is the Beast himself, really a 'prince in disguise' (as Nelly tells the boy he should consider himself rightly); Catherine's tragedy then was that she forgot her prince and he was forced to remain the monster, destroying her; invoking this pattern brought in much more from the fairy-tale world of magic, folk-lore and ballads, the oral tradition of the folk, that the Brontë children learnt principally from their nurses and their servant Tabby.[1] This element surges up in Chapter XII, the

[1] Tabby had, Mrs Gaskell reports, 'known the "bottom" or valley in those primitive days when the faeries frequented the margin of the "beck" on moonlight nights, and had known folk who had seen them. But that

important scene of Catherine's illness, where the dark superstitions about premonitions of death, about ghosts and primitive beliefs about the soul, come into play so significantly;[1] and again in the excessive attention given to Heathcliff's goblin-characteristics and especially to the prolonged account of his uncanny obsession and death. That this last should have an air of being infected by Hoffmann too is not surprising in a contemporary of Poe's; Emily is likely to have read Hoffmann when studying German at the Brussels boarding-school and certainly read the ghastly supernatural stories by James Hogg and others in the magazines at home. It is a proof of her immaturity at the time of the original conception of *Wuthering Heights* that she should express real psychological insights in such inappropriate forms.

In the novel as we read it Heathcliff's part either as Edmund in *Lear* or as the Prince doomed to Beast's form, is now suspended in boyhood while another influence, very much of the period, is developed, the Romantic image of childhood,[2] with a corresponding change of tone. Heathcliff and Catherine are idyllically and innocently happy together (and see also the end of Chapter V) roaming the countryside as hardy, primitive Wordsworthian children, 'half savage and hardy and free'. Catherine recalls it longingly when she feels she is dying trapped in Thrushcross Grange. (This boy Heathcliff is of course not assimilable with the vicious, scheming and morally heartless—'simply insensible'—boy of

was when there were no mills in the valleys, and when all the wool-spinning was done by hand in the farm-houses round. "It wur the factories as had driven 'em away", she said.'

[1] *v*. Appendix C.

[2] I am referring to the invaluable book, *The Image of Childhood*, by P. Coveney, though this does not in fact deal with *Wuthering Heights*.

Chapter IV who plays Edmund to old Earnshaw's Gloucester.) Catherine's dramatic introduction to the genteel world of Thrushcross Grange—narrated with contempt by Heathcliff who is rejected by it as a plough-boy unfit to associate with Catherine—is the turning-point in her life in *this* form of the novel; her return, got up as a young lady in absurdly unsuitable clothes for a farmhouse life, and 'displaying fingers wonderfully whitened with doing nothing and staying indoors'[1] etc. visibly separates her from the 'natural' life, as her inward succumbing to the temptations of social superiority and riches parts her from Heathcliff. Heathcliff's animus against his social degradation by his new master Hindley is barbed by his being made to suffer (like Pip at the hands of Estella in *Great Expectations*)[2] taunts and insults—mainly from Edgar Linton—based on class and externals

[1] This very evident judgment of Nelly's on the gentility with which Catherine has been infected by her stay at Thrushcross Grange (lavishly annotated in the whole scene of her return home in Chap. VII) is clearly endorsed by the author, since it is based on values that are fundamental to the novel and in consonance with Emily's Wordsworthian sympathies. It is supplemented by another similar but even more radical judgment, put into old Joseph's mouth, the indispensable Joseph who survives the whole action to go on farming the Heights and who is made the vehicle of several central judgments, as well as of many disagreeable Calvinistic attitudes. Resenting the boy Linton Heathcliff's contempt for the staple food, porridge, made, like the oat-cake, from the home-grown oats, Joseph remembers the boy's fine-lady mother: 'His mother were just soa—we wer a'most too mucky tuh sow t'corn fur makking her breead.' There are many related judgments in the novel. We may note here the near-caricature of Lockwood in the first three chapters as the town visitor continually exposing his ignorance of country life and farming.

[2] A regular Victorian theme, springing from the consciousness and resentment by creative artists of a new class snobbery and expressed in such widely different novels as *Alton Locke*, *North and South*, *Felix Holt*, *Dombey and Son*, *Great Expectations*, as well as *Wuthering Heights* which is earlier than all these.

alone. They are suffered again (thus making Emily Brontë's points inescapable) in the second half of the novel by Hindley's son Hareton at the hands of Catherine's and Edgar's daughter Cathy as well as from his other cousin Linton Heathcliff, Isabella's son. And this makes us sympathetic to Heathcliff as later to Hareton; we identify here with Nelly who with her wholesome classlessness and her spontaneous maternal impulses supports Heathcliff morally while he is ill-used (and even tries to persuade Catherine not to let Edgar supplant him in her life)—she retains this generous sympathy for him until she transfers it to her foster-child Hareton when in turn he becomes a victim (of Heathcliff's schemes). Her sympathy for Heathcliff's hard luck, even when she sees that his return is a threat to the Lintons' happiness, is at odds with her loyalty to her new master Edgar, and leads her to consent to some ill-advised interviews between Catherine and the desperate Heathcliff—though she also feels that to consent to help him there is the lesser of two evils (as it probably was), and she has no doubts about her duty to protect Isabella from becoming Heathcliff's victim.

Nelly Dean is most carefully, consistently and convincingly created for us as the normal woman, whose truly feminine nature satisfies itself in nurturing all the children in the book in turn.[1] To give this salience we have

[1] David Copperfield's Peggotty is the same type, registered through the nursling's eyes (she is supplemented, as he grows out of her, by his great-aunt Betsy Trotwood) and Dickens's testimony to such truths is important. It will be noticed that Peggotty has to mother not only David but also his permanently immature mother. Our nineteenth-century fiction and memoirs are full of such nurses (sometimes they are spinster aunts), bearing witness to the living reality (v., e.g., Lord Shaftesbury's nurse, the Strachey nurse, and the Darwin nurse in Gwen Raverat's autobiography

the beginning of Chapter VIII when the farm-girl runs out to the hayfield where Nelly is busy to announce the birth of 'a grand bairn' and to give her artless (normal feminine) congratulations to Nelly for being chosen to nurse it since it will soon be motherless: 'I wish I were you, because it will be all yours when there is no missus'. Nelly's greater sensibility in realizing that from the bairn's point of view this is not altogether a matter for rejoicing is shown in the next chapter when she says 'I went into the kitchen, and sat down to lull my little lamb to sleep ... I was rocking Hareton on my knee, and humming a song that began

> *"It was far in the night, and the bairnies grat,*
> *The mither beneath the mools heard that"* ...'

The ballad is evidently one expressing the widespread belief, in folk-song and folk tale, that a prematurely dead mother cannot rest in the grave but returns to suckle the babe or help her child in the hour of need,[1] an indication of what is going on in Nelly's compassionate mind. But the whole episode of Hareton's birth and childhood exposes Catherine's insensibility, that her self-centred nature is essentially loveless. (Her only reference to her own pregnancy later is the hope that a son's birth will 'erase Isabella's title' to be Edgar's heir.) Yet Nelly's

Period Piece). Nelly Dean seems to have incurred a good deal of unjustified ill-will, and perverse misrepresentation in consequence, from Catherine's defenders. That Peggotty and Miss Trotwood haven't (so far—or so far as I know) must be due less to Dickens's fairly unambiguous presentation of David's Dora and (but to a less degree) of David's mother, than to the fact that Doras are not now in esteem.

[1] Hence Nelly's indignant rebuke to Hareton's father in Chap. IX takes the form of telling him: ' "Oh! I wonder his mother does not rise from her grave to see how you use him".'

limitations are made clear and the novelist's distinct position of true insight, where necessary. Like Dolly in *Anna
Karénina* who is also the normal maternal woman, Nelly
is inevitably too *terre-à-terre* (Vronsky's complaint about
Dolly), therefore unable to sympathize with difficulties
that seem to her the result only of will, and a perverse
will at that (' "I should not have spoken so, if I had
known her true condition, but I could not get rid of the
notion that she acted a part of her disorder" '). These
limitations and not ill-will are of course the reason why
Nelly makes some mistakes in trying to act for the best
in situations where no easy or right solution offered itself.
But in doing Catherine full justice (' "she was not artful,
never played the coquette" ') and giving her sound advice
in her 'perplexities and untold troubles', Nelly convinces
us of her right to take a thoroughly disenchanted view of
Catherine's disposition. In fact, both Heathcliff and
Edgar know the truth about Catherine and Hindley is
under no illusions—' "You lie, Cathy, no doubt" ' he
remarks (correctly) of her explanation of Edgar Linton's
visit in his absence. One of the most successful indica-
tions of the passage of time is Nelly Dean's change, from
the quick-moving and quick-witted girl who for little
Hareton's sake copes with the drunken murderous
Hindley, to the stout, breathless, middle-aged woman
who, though still spirited, cannot save Cathy from a
forced marriage.

To hark back to Heathcliff: it follows from this 'social'
development of the theme that Heathcliff should go out
into the world to make his fortune and come back to
avenge himself, 'a cruel hard landlord', 'near, close-
handed' and given over to 'avarice, meanness and greed',
plotting to secure the property of both Earnshaws and

Lintons and also to claim equality with them socially—
we are now in the Victorian world of *Great Expectations*
where money, as Magwitch the convict learnt, makes a
gentleman. Emily Brontë took no trouble to explain the
hiatus in Heathcliff's life—irrelevant to her purposes—
and in fact it is enough for us to gather that he comes back
a professional gambler at cards; a real flaw however is
wholly inadequate illustration of the shared life and
interests of himself and Catherine that makes it plausible
that on his return she should be so absorbed in conversing
with him as to cut out immediately and altogether her
young husband. After all, we reflect, they couldn't always
have been talking about their childhood escapades—that
is to say, we recognize a failure in creative interest here
in the novelist; nor do we ever hear what they talk about
till Catherine attacks him over Isabella and they quarrel,
when it becomes clear even to Catherine that he can be
only the monster he has been made by his history. This
aspect of him is kept before us from now till the end
and accounts for his brutalities and violent outbreaks.
For various reasons, therefore, after envisaging several
alternative conceptions of Heathcliff, Emily Brontë ended
by keeping and making use of them all, so that like
Dostoievski's Stavrogin he is an enigmatic figure only by
reason of his creator's indecision, like Stavrogin in being
an unsatisfactory composite with empty places in his
history and no continuity of character. [And like Iago and
Stavrogin, Heathcliff has been made the object of much
misdirected critical industry on the assumption that he is
not merely a convenience.] There is nothing enigmatic
about either Catherine, we note, and this points to the
novelist's distribution of her interest.

There are various signs that the novelist intended to

stress the aspect of her theme represented by the corruption of the child's native goodness by Society and to make this part of the explanation of Catherine's failure in life. She evidently had in mind the difficulties and dangers inevitable in civilizing children to enter the artificial world of class, organized religion, social intercourse and authoritarian family life. This is the point of Catherine's childhood journal that Lockwood reads, which gives a caricature of the torments suffered by children in the enforcement of the Puritan Sabbath, and another caricature is the account given by the boy Heathcliff of the parlour life of the broken-in Linton children as seen from the other side of the window by a Noble Savage whose natural good instincts have not been destroyed like theirs. More impressive is the beautifully rendered exemplary relation between the child Catherine and the adults as reported by Nelly in Chapter V. Her father's attempts to improve her, or tame her to an approved pattern,[1] resulted only in 'a naughty delight to provoke him: she was never so happy as when we were all scolding her at once, and she defying us with her bold, saucy look, and her ready words; turning Joseph's religious curses into ridicule, baiting me, and doing just what her father hated most'— 'Mr. Earnshaw did not understand jokes from his children', Nelly notes, 'he had always been strict and grave with them'.

> 'After behaving as badly as possible all day, she sometimes came fondling to make it up at night. "Nay, Cathy" the old man would say, "I cannot love thee; go, say thy prayers, child, and ask God's pardon. I doubt thy mother and I must rue that we ever reared thee!" That made her cry, at first; and then,

[1] Significantly, because old Joseph 'was relentless in worrying him about ruling his children rigidly', as religion required.

being repulsed continually hardened her, and she laughed if I
told her to say she was sorry for her faults, and beg to be
forgiven. . . . It pleased the master rarely to see her gentle—
saying "Why canst thou not always be a good lass, Cathy?"
And she turned up her face to his, and laughed, and answered,
"Why cannot you always be a good man, father?" '

We note that the child is allowed the last word—and a
very telling rejoinder it is. Emily Brontë, the girl in the
family most sympathetic to the black-sheep brother, was
the most recalcitrant to the domestic training of her rigid
aunt, to schooling, and to orthodox religion; she had
plainly thought about the psychological effects of conventional disciplines and taken this opportunity to report
adversely in the strongest terms a novelist can use—by
showing their part in destroying the possibilities of a
happy childhood and maturity.

But this originally naïve and commonplace subject—
the Romantics' image of childhood in conflict with society
—becomes something that in this novel is neither super-
ficial nor theoretic because the interests of the responsible
novelist gave it, as we have seen above, a new insight, and
also a specific and informed sociological content. The
theme is here very firmly rooted in time and place and
richly documented: we cannot forget that Gimmerton and
the neighbourhood are so bleak that the oats are always
green there three weeks later than anywhere else, and that
old Joseph's Puritan preachings accompany his 'overlay-
ing his large Bible with dirty bank-notes, the produce of
the day's transactions' at market; and we have a thoroughly
realistic account of the life indoors and outdoors at
Wuthering Heights as well as at the gentleman's residence
at the Grange. In fact, there would be some excuse for
taking this, the pervasive and carefully maintained socio-

logical theme which fleshes the skeleton, for the real novel. This novel, which could be extracted by cutting away the rest, was deliberately built, to advance a thesis, on the opposition between Wuthering Heights and Thrushcross Grange, two different cultures of which the latter inevitably supersedes the former. The point about dating this novel as ending in 1801 (instead of its being contemporary with the Brontës' own lives)—and much trouble was taken to keep the dates, time-scheme and externals such as legal data, accurate[1]—is to fix its happenings at a time when the old rough farming culture based on a naturally patriarchal family life, was to be challenged, tamed and routed by social and cultural changes that were to produce the Victorian class consciousness and 'unnatural' ideal of gentility.[2]

The inspiration for this structure, based on a conflict between, roughly speaking, a wholesome primitive and natural unit of a healthy society and its very opposite, felt to be an unwholesome refinement of the parasitic 'educated', comes from observation—in the Brontës' youth and county the old order visibly survived [v. Appendix A]. But the clue to making such perceptions and sympathies into a novel was found, I suspect, in Scott, whose novels and poetry were immensely admired by Charlotte and Emily. His own sympathies were with

[1] v. C. P. Sanger's *The Structure of 'Wuthering Heights'* (a Hogarth Press pamphlet).

[2] Other pre-Victorian novelists noted and resented the effects on children too. In the original preface to her children's classic *Holiday House* (1839), Catherine Sinclair wrote: 'In these pages the author has endeavoured to paint that species of noisy, frolicsome, mischievous children, now almost extinct, wishing to preserve a sort of fabulous remembrance of days long past, when young people were like wild horses on the prairies, rather than like well-broken hacks on the road.'

the wild rough Border-farmers, not only because they
represented a romantic past of balladry. He felt that
civilization introduced there entailed losses more than
gains, and a novel where—before, with characteristic
lack of staying power, he divagated from a serious theme
into tushery—he made some effort to express this, *The
Black Dwarf*, has long been known as the source for
surnames used in *Wuthering Heights*. Scott's Earnscliffe
[=Eaglescliff] and Ellieslaw suggested Heathcliff[1] and
Earnshaw no doubt, but more important is their suggesting, it seems to me, that Emily Brontë found part of
her theme in that novel's contrast between a weak, cor-
rupt, refined upper-class, and the old-style Border farmers'
'natural' or socially primitive way of life in which feuds
and violence were a recognized part of the code (though
transacted for the most part strictly according to rule and
tradition and quite compatible with good-humour and a
generous humanity); there, the rich and great live in
their castles, are treacherous, and come to grief, the rough
Borderers, eking out subsistence farming by hunting,
suffer drastic ups and downs with hardihood and survive;
the setting is on the moors and hills, and an essential
element in establishing the primitive social condition of
the Borderers is the superstition and folk-lore believed in
by them all. Now the Yorkshire moors with the hardy
yeomen farmers of pre-Victorian times who had lived
thereabouts and whose histories Tabby used to tell the
Brontë children[2] in her broad dialect, must have seemed

[1] With the added force of Scott's dark and violent *Ravenswood* who
both in name-pattern and type of hero suggests Heathcliff. *v*. Appendix D,
'*Wuthering Heights* and *The Bride of Lammermoor*'.

[2] Mrs Gaskell says she told 'of bygone days of the countryside; old ways
of living, former inhabitants, decayed gentry who had melted away, and
whose places knew them no more; family tragedies, and dark superstitious

to them not essentially different from Scott's Border farmers. Emily and Charlotte were genuinely attached to their moorland country but Scott's example was what made it usable for them as literature and gave it rich associations, so it is natural that in her first attempt at a novel Emily should draw on even a poor fiction like *The Black Dwarf* to give meaning and purpose to her feelings about what was happening or had happened recently to the world she lived in. It is proof of her development out of her daydream world of the Gondals that she was thus interested in the real world and roused to the need to inquire into the true nature of the change, perhaps as a way to alert her own (Early Victorian) generation to what this was. From being a self-indulgent storytelling, *Wuthering Heights* thus became a responsible piece of work, and the writer thought herself into the positions, outlooks, sufferings and tragedies of the actors in these typical events as an *artist*.

But if we were to take the sociological novel as the real novel and relegate the Heathcliff-Catherine-Edgar relationship and the corresponding Cathy-Linton-Hareton one, as exciting but ex-centric dramatic episodes, we should be misconceiving the novel and slighting it, for it is surely these relationships and their working out that give all the meaning to the rest. For instance, though Cathy has in the second half to unlearn, very painfully, the assumptions of superiority on which she has been brought up at the Grange, this is only part of her schooling; it is only incidental to the process by which we see

dooms; and in telling these things, without the least consciousness that there might ever be anything requiring to be softened down, would give at full length the bare and simple details.' This is evidence of external, real life, sources for *Wuthering Heights* which cannot be dismissed.

her transcend the psychological temptations and the impulses which would have made her repeat her mother's history; and this is not a question of sociology or social history but is timeless.

Another misconception for which the novelist gives little excuse is to attribute a mystique to the moor; the moor is not meaningful like Hawthorne's forests that surround the Puritan settlements in the wild, it is not even powerful over man's destiny like Egdon Heath. The moor is a way of pointing a distinction: to the child Cathy brought up in the gentleman's park at the Grange, the moor means freedom from restraint, and romantic Nature to which she longs to escape, and in which she delights, but to the people who live there of necessity it is something they have to wrest a living out of: in the long run man lives by farming, and the farmhouse at the Heights is braced against the challenge the extreme conditions there represent (for instance, on our first sight of it we see that the architecture is determined by the violence of the winds). Lockwood (characteristically) demands that the farm should provide him with a guide home when, though snow threatened, he foolishly paid a call, and he thinks, as we at first do, that the refusal is brutal and wanton; but there is no guide to spare—the hands are needed to get in the sheep before the animals are snowed under and to see to the horses. Similarly, when Cathy in her thoughtlessness uses her new power over Hareton to get him to pull up the fruit-bushes to make her a flower-garden, old Joseph, who has worked all his life at the Heights and meant to die there, is so outraged that he gives notice rather than stay to witness such a sinful proceeding as to sacrifice food to flowers. Unattractive as Joseph usually is, his disinterested identification with the family's well-being is impressive and as so often he is the vehicle for expressing a truth to which we need to have our attention called: here, that where fertile soil is precious, flower-gardens are an unjustified self-indulgence. Another example (there are plenty) is Linton Heathcliff's selfishness, due like Cathy's to ignorance of the facts of life on such a farm: Zillah complains 'he must always have sweets and dainties, and always milk, milk for ever—heeding naught how the rest of us are pinched in winter'. The novelist knows that thrift as well as austerity is a necessary virtue in such a context, so that old Joseph's indignation when the feckless Isabella flings down the tray of porridge is wholly respectable: '"yah desarve pining froo this tuh Churstmas, flinging t'precious gifts uh God under fooit i' yer flaysome rages!"'

The clearest light is thrown on the moor by Catherine's likening Heathcliff to 'an arid wilderness of furze and whinstone' when trying to make the romantic Isabella understand the basic irreducibility of the nature of the man Isabella fancies she is in love with. But Catherine has also said to Nelly, in trying to explain her own 'love' for Heathcliff, that it is like 'the eternal rocks: a source of little visible delight, but necessary,' in fact it is not love but a need of some fundamental kind that is quite separate from her normal love for Edgar Linton, a love which leads to a happily consummated marriage and the expectation of providing an heir.

The focus of the first half of the novel is most certainly Catherine, and it is her case that is the real moral centre of the book. This case is examined with wonderful subtlety and conveyed in a succession of brilliantly managed dramatic scenes with complete impersonality. Charlotte Brontë rightly defended her sister against allegations of

abnormality by pointing out that, as well as what Charlotte
justly describes as 'the perverted passion and passionate
perversity' of the first Catherine, and Heathcliff's 'warped
nature', Emily had created the wholesome, maternal Nelly
Dean, Edgar Linton's touching devotion and tenderness,
and the 'grace and gaiety' of the younger Cathy—she
might have instanced much more. And what precisely is
this case, in which—and not in the sociological novel,
which is more a matter of course in its age—lies the real
originality of *Wuthering Heights*? Here I think we can
draw very usefully on a remarkable modern novel, *Jules
et Jim* by Henri-Pierre Roché. The film is more widely
known that François Truffaud made from it—so intelligently that the film can serve the purpose for those
who haven't read the book.[1] I should have thought the
resemblance of the plot and theme of the film to the core
of the first half of *Wuthering Heights* was very striking,
but the novel is still more like, while providing, in its
challenging modernity and absence of all that makes it
possible to describe *Wuthering Heights* as a regional novel,
a means of showing critically why the older novel is more
important and interesting. I must therefore use not the
film but Roché's novel (pub. Gallimard, 1953). After a
diffuse start it becomes the record of relations developing
between two men and a woman (Kate, though confusingly

[1] In general, the film wipes out inessentials and makes the theme
inescapable; it telescopes with advantage, translates intellectual elements
successfully into dramatic forms while wherever possible exactly re-
producing the original, and interpolates very little. It is a faithful rendition
which shirks almost nothing—unlike the usually over-praised 'film of the
novel', or dramatised version (contrast the film of the novel *Saturday
Night and Sunday Morning*, which both softens and shirks, or the dreadful
play *The Heiress* which misinterprets and denatures *Washington Square*).
Nevertheless, this film omits the physical violence of the novel and is thus
more suave and less disturbing than Roché's work.

—for *Wuthering Heights* purposes—named Catherine in the film). Kate answers exactly to Charlotte Brontë's description above of Catherine Earnshaw as well as in nearly all other essentials—it seems not to matter that, living in a sexually permissive society (twentieth-century Germany and France) she takes full licence, for she ends in Catherine's situation, and endures and causes similar suffering. Jules whom she marries is gentle, with bookish and philosophic leanings, like Edgar Linton, while Jim, a writer, is passionate, hard and violent, providing for Kate something that she needs to keep her alive and whole that her husband lacks—though she can't do without what Jules stands for either. Acquiescent as Jules inevitably is, considering the sophisticated society in which they live, and even by choice since his deep friendship with Jim antedates their meeting with Kate, and also because he hopes that, Jim being for Kate a lover who supplements himself in temperament, his marriage will be saved (he has two little girls)—yet the situation is inherently disastrous and ends with Kate's destroying herself and dragging the not unwilling Jim with her, while Jules survives, like Edgar Linton, only to foster his little daughters.

Except for the bond between the two men, the likeness to the first part of the English novel is obvious—and enlightening as to Emily Brontë's intentions in developing out of a simple sociological conflict an original psychological exploration. One would assume that the later (French) novel might have been based on the earlier (English) one, and that Lawrence's *Women in Love* also provided a model for Roché (one sees that Lawrence's respect for *Wuthering Heights* must have owed something to its usefulness for him). To check this I wrote to M.

Roché (in 1964) only to find that he had died a few years before at the age of eighty, and that the events in his apparently very contemporary novel which are there placed in the years 1911–1930 did actually take place then. Mme Roché kindly assured me that the novel was in fact written up from the daily journal her husband kept, during those years, of his personal history (before she knew him), written up long after, when they were refugees during the last war and without the journal at hand, but still closely following the journal, as she can testify. He did rewrite the novel three times at intervals (no doubt to achieve greater impersonality, though at the start of the novel particularly the shapelessness of life confuses the reader). Mme Roché informed me also that though he had read *Wuthering Heights*, and probably *Women in Love*, she thinks it would have been *after* the events recorded in his diary and which are reproduced in *Jules et Jim*, nor does she think he was influenced by *any* literary work in this composition.

There are no distractions in *Jules et Jim* to prevent us seeing that it is a psychological drama written with an almost clinical detachment; both it and the film (in which Kate is fairly adequately embodied by Jeanne Moreau) achieved notoriety as an astonishing case-history. No mystical explanation is needed for Kate, and we can therefore see that none is needed for Catherine Earnshaw —though it is natural that at that date Emily Brontë should feel obliged to provide something of the kind, and inevitable that it should take the form of not very impressive rhetoric (in Chapter IX, ' "If all else perished and *he* remained" ' etc., and elsewhere). Natural too that Emily Brontë should have had difficulty in explaining even to herself her genuine insights and that she should be driven to attach, to the delicately truthful notation of them in action and dialogue, explanations of them as 'poetry', a prose rhetoric of declamation which is in resonance with much that is unsatisfactory in the rhetorical verse of the Gondal cycle.[1] It is very unfortunate that the brief, and on the whole misleading, 'metaphysical' parts of *Wuthering Heights* should have been not only over-rated but universally seized on as a short cut to the meaning, the significance of the novel (to the virtual exclusion of the real novel enacted so richly for us to grasp in all its complexity). We might consider as a related weakness Heathcliff's mainly melodramatic explanations of himself, Heathcliff being made up of so many inconsistent parts that the novelist evidently was in some perplexity to make him cohere enough to make an impressive final appearance and exit. [In contrast to her carelessness about Heathcliff we must note the care she took to make plausible Lockwood's burying himself at Thrushcross Grange, being kept there by illness to hear Nelly's long narration, and returning for the conclusion of the Linton-Earnshaw history, as also her providing an explanation of Nelly's being more sensitive and better educated than an ordinary housekeeper, as she needs to be.] A weakness arising out of this is the disproportionate space allotted to Heathcliff's final lapse into the desire to die in order to join Catherine and the disintegration of his

[1] For the nature of the rhetoric, *v. Scrutiny*, Vol. XIX, No. 2, F. R. Leavis: 'Reality and Sincerity', where the poem 'Cold in the earth' is analysed in a comparison with a poem by Thomas Hardy. [Reprinted in *A Selection From Scrutiny*, Vol. II.] Systematic attempts to argue that the Gondal poems are the basis of *Wuthering Heights* provide a harmless academic pastime, but we have only to ask whether, the novel being lost, we could have deduced anything even remotely resembling it from the poems, to see how preposterous the claim is.

will; and another is the occasional flirtation with the juvenile conception of him as possessed by the Devil. [There are, however, two places where this idea is given temporary justification: one is the momentary appearance of Heathcliff 'on the door stones' which makes Nelly, who has come to fight for the interests of little Hareton, lose her nerve and rush away 'as if I had raised a goblin', the other is Joseph's account, of how Heathcliff is deliberately ruining Catherine's brother, in what might be a passage from the *Pilgrim's Progress*: ' "I' course, he tells Dame Catherine hah hor father's son gallops dahn t'Broad road, while he flees afore tuh oppen t'pikes?" ']

To return to the argument from *Jules et Jim*: as Kate's history was taken from an actuality there is no reason why an observer of genius should not have deduced and composed Catherine Earnshaw from reported or observed real life, for her behaviour is essentially that of Roché's Kate, though whereas M. Roché was personally an actor in his drama it is certain that Emily Brontë had no such first-hand facilities. There is less felt anguish in her novel than in his in consequence, but more useful insight. This is proved by her adding the second half to her novel, instead of leaving us with a case on our hands—though one which M. Roché's diary shows to have been a human possibility and in fact a not unrepresentative one once one recognizes that the kind of woman of which Catherine Earnshaw and Kate are specimens is not uncommon.[1] Inevitably, since the Romantics had made Love

[1] What might be called the Catherine complex did not go unnoticed by other Victorian novelists. Mrs Gaskell, who had a sound knowledge of the dialects and culture of her own parts of England, had thought of introducing into her novel *North and South* a young girl from 'humble, retired country life on the borders of Lancashire' to be angry, jealous and passionately in love with the hero—'I know', she wrote in this connexion,

between man and woman the focus of values, succeeding novelists were led to ask what in terms of daily life does love become. Roché's novel, though consummations of love frequently occur in it, is not about sex, any more than *Women in Love* is: it is entirely an examination, in Jim's words, of 'what people call love'. Emily Brontë seems to have been equally occupied with this problem though as a much finer artist she saw it in all its complexity. Kate is a woman who uses her exceptional attractions to dominate men, humiliate them, punish them, or reward them if they obey her, and is jealously possessive of their persons and their inner selves too while demanding the right to retain complete liberty herself. Like a

Letter No. 191, 'the kind of wild, wayward character that grows up in lonesome places, which has a sort of Southern capacity of hating and loving.' Dickens's Rosa Dartle, perhaps his most interesting female, registers his recognition of the woman with whom something has gone wrong so that her passionate nature must vent itself in destructive rages against those necessary to her. The only outlet Rosa's restricted life allows is a practice of undermining everyone by ironical questioning (the hint from real life on which Dickens built the character); her face is scarred from a hammer thrown at her by the young Steerforth (whom she has always loved passionately) owing to her having goaded him to such exasperation—symbolic of their relation to each other. But Miss Dartle is only a minor character in *David Copperfield*, and Dickens seems unable to do anything with it beyond a few impressive sketches of her in action. Further thinking on those lines presumably produced Miss Wade in *Little Dorrit*. She has been impelled to break off her approaching marriage (an excellent love-match), and later also a *liaison* with a cynical pseudo-artist who supplemented the worthy fiancé, because she can maintain no relation requiring love and self-discipline; she is actually shown most convincingly creating around herself finally a *Huits Clos* life of destructive passion and self-torment quite equal to the vortex set up by Catherine. Both Rosa Dartle and Miss Wade are clever, handsome and highly-sexed, but have been put into disadvantageous positions by life—the one is a poor relation, the other illegitimate, and both are resentful, so that like Catherine (but unlike Roché's Kate) they are accounted for by circumstances in their early conditioning.

child, she assumes she is the centre of the world and has no sense of responsibility. Her power lies not in crude sex but in being, like Catherine Earnshaw, a dazzling original character whose personality enchants because she is able to make sunshine and happiness for everyone around her if she can only be kept contented.[1] Though there are in the background of Roché's novel other women, they are all neutralised by or summarized in her (Jules and Jim call her 'the queen bee'), so that we conclude that Kate is not offered as a perverse or dangerous woman but as WOMAN in essence, a menace to masculine stability and man's achievement of a civilized code, and yet indispensable to any life worth living—I take it this is the point of that 'archaic smile' which gets such a lot of stress in the novel and symbolizes the archaic characteristics which in spite of the dangers they imply are what Roché thinks men seek in a woman and which are seen to be stronger than men's civilized selves. Kate is shown as absolutely hostile to man-made rules: she cheats, steals without any reason, tells lies shamelessly, rejoices in violent scenes, acts on intuition always, refuses to admit any moral law except a childish tit-for-tat which always has to work in her own interest, and has no patience with

[1] Catherine Earnshaw is well in line here, e.g. 'Mr Linton ventured no objection to her taking Isabella with her to Wuthering Heights in the afternoon; and she rewarded him with such a summer of sweetness and affection in return, as made the house a paradise for several days; both master and servants profiting from the perpetual sunshine.' And even in the first phase of the marriage: 'It was not the thorn bending to the honeysuckles but the honeysuckles embracing the thorn. There were no mutual concessions: one stood erect, and the others yielded ... I observed that Mr Edgar had a deep-rooted fear of ruffling her humour. He concealed it from her; ... and for the space of half a year, the gunpowder lay as harmless as sand, because no fire came near to explode it. ... It ended. ...'

the masculine world of logic, reason and impersonal justice (though she is no fool and has literary and artistic ability). When she is ill, generally through her wilful bouts of passion, she demands devotion from men, but is unfeeling and irritated when they fall ill. What she cannot and will not bear is that men should escape from her into their world of intellectual interests. It is the first meeting between the friends after her marriage when they insist on discussing their work, ignoring her, that makes her take the desperate step of jumping into the Seine and swimming underwater to alarm her husband into submission (tough-minded Jim is unmoved except by admiration)—this is also a forecast of her last desperate bid for power when seeing Jim about to escape from her by marriage she deliberately drives their car into the Seine to drown him with her.

Now, not only does Catherine Earnshaw behave similarly and often identically, she has even the same disgust for her husband's bookishness, which she identifies as the source of his weakness or inadequacy. It is true the Lintons seem to shrink from healthy outdoor life and prefer to get their ideas about life from literature (in Isabella's case leading to her disastrous infatuation with Heathcliff conceived as a sensitive, noble Byronic soul—Catherine knows better); and that Wordsworth's mistrust of books and meddling intellect apparently gives respectable support to Catherine's attitude. But it is also apparent that Catherine feels her husband's intellectual tastes to be rivals—when intolerably provoked by her he retires to his studies, and it is this she thinks of when, on what she feels to be her death-bed, she envisages him with great bitterness as ' "offering prayers of thanks to God for restoring peace to his house, and going back to his

books!" '. The Emily Brontë who kneaded the dough
with a German book propped up before her cannot be
supposed to endorse Catherine's hostility to learning;
and though we must beware of identifying the novelist's
attitude to Catherine with Nelly's, yet in general she
endorses Nelly's shrewd analysis of Catherine's behaviour.
Unlike Nelly however the novelist though concerned to
diagnose does not blame Catherine, because she under-
stands, as Nelly cannot, why a Catherine can hardly help
behaving as she does. But she is as far as possible from
admiring Catherine; being a woman, Emily Brontë has
none of Roché's fascinated respect for his Kate as a force
of nature. The woman novelist does not believe that all
women share these characteristics more or less and are
unfeminine without them, in fact, she takes pains to show
that these characteristics are incompatible with what is
required of a wife and mother. On the other hand, Roché's
strength lies in being able to evoke a civilization made by
the efforts of men which is indestructible by Woman.
The friendship between the two men who have been
students together and have in common a devotion to
literature and the arts, though they are of different
nationalities, a friendship which, to make the point clear,
is shown as surviving even their fighting on opposite
sides in the first World War as well their being in love
with the same woman—this is the point in which *Jules
et Jim* is more subtle than *Wuthering Heights*, where the
ill-will between Edgar and Heathcliff is dramatically
commonplace. [Of course their hostility was necessary
also in the sociological context of the novel where Edgar's
assurance of class superiority and the unfeeling social
contempt Heathcliff is exposed to in adolescence condition Heathcliff to become the Frankenstein monster we

are introduced to by Mr Lockwood at the opening of the novel. Even so, Emily Brontë struggles to suggest some deeper truths than the situation seems to hold: for instance, Heathcliff's protestation to Nelly that he is superior to mere rivalry for Catherine's love—' "had he been in my place and I in his, though I hated him with a hatred that turned my life to gall, I never would have raised a hand against him. I never would have banished him from her society as long as she desired his. . . . I would have died by inches before I touched a single hair of his head!" ']

Over and above their hostility, Catherine deliberately foments trouble between them as part of her need for violence and domination; and the scene where she locks the three of them in and then throws the key on the fire, putting her delicate (though by no means cowardly) husband at the mercy of the brutal Heathcliff, and humiliating him by her insults, disloyalty and indifference to what happens to him, is extremely painful reading. She has no moral sensibility to comprehend that he is stricken not by cowardice but by her attitude to him. In these ways she behaves quite as insufferably as Kate but unlike her she is offset in the context of the novel by many other and very different feminine natures and dispositions,[1] this point being driven home in the second half where the younger Catherine, with similar drives and temptations to her mother's, is able to profit by experience and get a moral education from her sufferings because she is also her father's daughter. It is the men who strike one as making a consistently poor showing in *Wuthering Heights*—not only Heathcliff and his odious son Linton

[1] In *Wuthering Heights* there is a much greater range of feminine types than in either *Jules et Jim* or *Women in Love,* for example.

but the generally callous Joseph, the misguided older Earnshaw, his drunken son Hindley, the crude youth Hareton, the conceited narrator Lockwood, and even Edgar Linton who is imprisoned in class and for all his civilized virtues ineffective. But in spite of these inevitable differences in prejudice by a male and a female novelist, there is a wide agreement in Roché's and Emily Brontë's investigations into 'what people call love'. Both isolate the striking irrationality that impels the heroine of each to destroy her own possibility of happiness, both note that the only kind of love a woman like Catherine or Kate can feel is death-centred. A surprising insight of Emily Brontë's is that apportioning moral blame is impossible. Nelly Dean after describing the precarious nature of the Linton's married happiness says:

> ' "It ended. Well, we *must* be for ourselves in the long run; the mild and the generous are only more justly selfish than the domineering; and it ended when circumstances caused each to feel that the one's interest was not the chief consideration in the other's thoughts." '

This is a basic truth, that the identification of interests in marriage is the only way of getting over the conflict of egos. Heathcliff's return is the spark that set off the train of gunpowder, but something else would have done so otherwise. Later on, in Edgar's tender devotion to Catherine in her final illness and even mental decay, we get another answer to the inquiry, "What is it that people call Love?"; this answer is not cynical. But Catherine, like Kate, is shown to be incapable of love in this sense—' "I care nothing for your sufferings. Why shouldn't you suffer? I do," ' she says to Heathcliff in their last interview—and Heathcliff justly says of her haunting spirit, as her husband might equally have done:

' "She showed herself, as she often was in life, a devil to me." ' Even when Heathcliff is taking farewell of the dying Catherine he upbraids her with her 'infernal selfishness'. In fact, the scenes between Catherine and Heathcliff after his return are the climax of the novel as regards establishing this theme; so thoroughly is the author determined to develop them that she hardly troubles to bring them about naturally, thus exposing Nelly to charges of connivance or worse.

But though *Jules et Jim* is an unforgettable novel, it belongs for me in the *Adolphe* class—something I hardly want to read again because with all its genuineness it gives so much more discomfort than satisfaction. And compared with *Wuthering Heights* it is a novel of so much less interest, in spite of its freedom from a Victorian novelist's limitations in dealing with sex (which nevertheless, in *Wuthering Heights*, are not a handicap). Why does one feel that in spite of its intensely painful scenes— painful in a great variety of ways—*Wuthering Heights* always repays rereading? It is easy to lay a finger on a passage that shows why what only disturbs in *Jules et Jim* moves us profoundly in the other novel, because instead of a clinical presentation we get a delicate annotation of behaviour that convinces us that it is not perverse but natural, human and inevitable. Take the sequence (Chapter VIII) when Catherine at fifteen is transferring her interest (unintentionally) from the now degraded Heathcliff to Edgar Linton, who besides being a desirable match does genuinely represent standards she must admire, even though it is a strain for her to have to appear to share them. We are actually shown her suffering from this strain and what the consequences are. Expecting Edgar, she has ungraciously to get rid of Heathcliff who

hangs about her, and so she is already out of temper
because uneasy about her treatment of her childhood
friend. Consequently she is spitefully cross with Nelly
who (on orders from the master) thwarts her desire to
be alone with Edgar, is driven to defend herself to Edgar
by a patent fib, then to laying hands in temper on her
little nephew who naturally supports his foster-mother,
and then when Edgar interferes to rescue the child she
instinctively boxes *his* ear, in an irresistible progress of
passion. Edgar, 'greatly shocked at the double fault of
falsehood and violence which his idol has committed',
reasons with her, but to reason she has no answer.

> Catherine was mute.
> 'And you told a deliberate untruth!', he said. 'I didn't!' she
> cried, recovering her speech; 'I did nothing deliberately.'

To him, telling a lie and striking him in a most unlady-
like way are serious offences, as well as quarrelling with a
servant (Nelly—to him always 'Ellen') and ill-treating a
child. To her (as to Roché's Kate) that her behaviour was
spontaneous justified it ("I did nothing deliberately").
She is not ashamed of being herself, having no such
standards and no image of correct behaviour as he has
which he feels obliged to sustain. She continues: ' "Well,
go if you please—get away. And now I'll cry—I'll cry
myself sick" ', and she proceeds to do so. If he is unjust
enough to blame her for what she can't help she will
punish him by making herself ill, a child's revenge and
self-protective technique—' "She set to weeping in
serious earnest" ' Nelly reports then. What is pardonable
at fifteen becomes, however, the pattern of her mode of
domination ('falsehood and violence'), leading her when
married to starve herself into delirium, threaten suicide,

and look forward to death as a release[1] from an intolerable self as well as from an intolerable situation, destroying also in effect both the men who love her. And this self is not archaic Woman like Roché's Kate but is shown in growth as the product of strains in social and emotional life in childhood and adolescence. Jules placates Kate because he 'considers her as a natural force expressing itself through cataclysms'—this seems too pompous and to explain nothing; the superior sophistication of the French intellectual, the artists' world in which Roché's novel is set, and the complete lack of any moral code (except that of 'enlightenment') in any of the characters, are seen to be disadvantages because there is really no moral interest, only a series of shocks and surprises. Even the surprises in *Wuthering Heights* though not showy are much more rewarding ultimately. The scene I've just summarized between the young people ends by Nelly's noting that though she urged Edgar to 'take warning and be gone' (both for his own sake and in Heathcliff's interests), he couldn't:

> 'The soft thing looked askance through the window. He possessed the power to depart, as much as a cat possesses the power to leave a mouse half killed, or a bird half eaten.'

The surprise is that 'the soft thing' (soft applying to his nature and not to the cat's—with which he is surprisingly identified—but only to the cat's furry exterior, which is a shock in itself) Edgar, is not compared as one would expect with the mouse or bird, but with the cat that kills

[1] Not merely as a release, but, characteristically, she must represent it as a triumph: ' "Nelly, you think you are better and more fortunate than I; in full health and strength: you are sorry for me—very soon that will be altered. I shall be sorry for *you*. I shall be incomparably beyond and above you all." '

and eats them, a double shock. [Later on this is underlined by Joseph's referring to 'yon cat uh Linton'.]. This surprise when we register it makes us realize a new truth, that a cat is really a victim of drives it can't resist too[1] (just as, later, we learn that 'the mild and generous' are just as selfish as 'the domineering' because they too '*must* be for themselves in the long run'—a law of nature). Moreover it obliges us to compassionate Catherine who is, justly, identified with the mouse or bird that Edgar the cat will catch and consume; she is pathetic because she is helpless before Edgar's fascination for her as someone who represents a finer social life and moral type than she has been used to, even though marrying him will be, as Heathcliff points out too late, like planting an oak in a flower-pot. A final surprise and another psychological truth is Nelly's observation that this scene had an opposite effect to what might have been expected: 'the quarrel had merely effected a closer intimacy—had broken the outworks and enabled them to confess themselves lovers'.

And this episode (Chap. VIII, that is) not only leads inevitably to Catherine's self-destruction; it is recalled by contrast when we read the scene in Chapter XI where Nelly goes up to the Heights to see how her foster-child Hareton is getting on and to warn his father, her old playmate Hindley, against Heathcliff. Full of tender reminiscences of their joint childhood, she comes on the child Hareton, whom she at first takes for his father a generation

---

[1] Other insights of the same kind are that Heathcliff's worst potentialities are roused by what Nelly describes as Cathy's 'accustomed look of nervousness, and yet defiance, which he abhorred', and also by Isabella's combination of the hated Linton looks with her fatuous delusions about himself, (which reminds one of Byron's reactions to poor Annabella both before and after marriage).

ago, to find, to her horror and ours, that he has forgotten his foster-mother completely and, schooled by Heathcliff, greets her with curses and stones. With the most admirable restraint she suppresses her natural reactions, even grief, to try to do something for the child's welfare. Recalling Catherine's behaviour ('wicked aunt Cathy') to the same child, we realise that Catherine's kind of femininity is neither exhaustive of the possibilities of Woman nor really typical. And Nelly's adult and selflessly maternal behaviour prepares us for her foster-child's, the younger Catherine's, evolution away from the possibilities of repeating her mother's disaster, though Cathy is shown to have similar impulses and in some ways nearly as unfortunate an upbringing (she is everyone's idol at the Grange). Cathy achieves the self-knowledge and wisdom that bring her to a successful coming of age as a woman with which the novels ends. Roché's novel and Truffaud's film with equal and unnecessary pessimism show Kate's daughter committed in childhood to an instinctive repetition of the mother's attitudes. Their message seems to be '*Così fan tutte*'.

It is quite otherwise in *Wuthering Heights*, where a careful integrity of observation and a finer, more informed insight, are apparent. We may note the care taken to make conventional moral judgments impossible (its original readers would have been only too inclined to make them) by showing always the psychological reasons for certain kinds of behaviour, so that there is nothing mysterious or incredible about Catherine or even, in essentials, about Heathcliff. And it is important to realize that the principal events are made to take place in the early adolescence of all the main actors, when they are so young as to be at the mercy of their impulses. Also (as we should

have realized even if the actors and actions were not transmitted to us through the critical medium of Mr Lockwood
who is so conscious of being stuck in a half-savage
country) the time is the eighteenth century and the place
remote and northern. The unconscious brutality of the
family doctor who, telling Hindley that his wife is dying,
adds: 'It can't be helped. And besides, you should have
known better than to choose such a rush of a lass!' is an
early index of the northern plain speaking that is proud
of putting sense in place of feeling.[1] [Zillah fills this post
in the second half of the novel.] But after the shock this
gives us, we realize it is truth and an important truth in
the world of the Heights. A farmer's wife, especially in
such testing conditions, needed to be robust to do what
was required and provide healthy children. By choosing
a delicate lass Hindley was flouting traditional wisdom
(as the doctor points out)—fatally. He had gone to
college (we now see why he was made to) and acquired an
unsuitable taste in women, for which he must now pay;
Nature is ruthless too. And in such ways the sociological
element or setting of the book is indispensable, in re-
inforcing these radical truths on which life has to be built.

[1] The economy and impersonality with which this point is made, and
the complexity of apprehension—so that what seems gratuitously wound-
ing is seen to be also natural (i.e. necessary) in the context of such a way
of life—contrasts, greatly to Emily's advantage, with Charlotte's raw
reaction to the same Yorkshire plain-speaking, as seen in *Shirley*. There
Emily's sister presents a whole family (drawn from life), given the typical
name of 'the Yorkes', to show the hurtful effect of this much-vaunted 'out-
spokenness'; Charlotte has the father and mother 'told off' by both heroines,
making an obtrusively personal episode which is not integral to the novel.
Charlotte, that is, could see only the disagreeable effects of this northern
characteristic, whereas Emily understood and made clear the reasons why
it came about and prevailed, since, as she shows, it made for survival
originally, though of course unnecessary to the Linton class now.

It is what gives Emily Brontë an immeasurable advantage over Roché. For when it is finally borne in on Jim that any sustained relation between Kate and Jules or between Kate and himself is hopeless, he reflects that this break-down 'might have been avoided if Kate and he had belonged to the same race and religion, or if Kate and Jules had, but as things were they could only speak to each other ultimately in translation. Words hadn't exactly the same sense for them both, not even gestures; their notions of order, authority, the part played by man and woman, were all different.' This is because Jim was French and Catholic, Kate German and Protestant, and Jules a German Jew. We are *told* so, but we have never had these differences, so basic, acted out or decisively indicated. The corresponding differences between the farm-house culture of Wuthering Heights and the polite world of Thrushcross Grange in social attitudes, instinctive behaviour, physical appearance and health, style of speech, way of living, dress, deportment, emotional habits —the whole idiom of life—are perpetually kept before us and are given their due importance in determining action, plot and characterization. Even the difference between both these orders and the fashionable society of city and watering-place from which Lockwood takes his tone, is never forgotten (brought out afresh at the opening of Chapter XXXII when Lockwood pays his final visit to the Heights). Isabella's illusions which lead to her wretched marriage are as characteristic of the over-sheltered life at the Grange as the lung-disease from which all the Lintons die except Catherine's daughter (who is half an Earnshaw). The importance of the sociological content of the novel to the novelist is proved by her pains to show Heathcliff's eventual regrets about his enemies' son Hareton, only because Hareton's wounded feelings (due to the position Heathcliff has deliberately placed him in) remind him of his own embittered youth as the uncouth ploughboy; he never softens to Cathy, the child of his other enemy, though she is also the daughter of his beloved Catherine and has suffered more at his hands than Hareton.

Yet though *Wuthering Heights* is concerned to replace moralistic judgment by compassionate understanding, it has a very firm moral effect. The technical means invented by Emily Brontë for implying moral criticism without stating it, for making the reader do this work himself, is the technique of contrast and parallelism. I have indicated some of these passages already which we are intended to take note of in this way, though of course the whole novel is really constructed on this principle, in its two complementary halves. In the second half, to which I've hitherto given little attention, there is a very striking example, in Zillah's narrative (Chapter XXX) reported by Nelly. After the forced marriage Cathy has been shut up at the Heights to take care of her diseased young husband. She having asked 'all in a quiver' for a doctor as 'her cousin was very ill':

> ' "We know that!" answered Heathcliff; "but his life is not worth a farthing, and I won't spend a farthing on him."
>
> "But I cannot tell how to do," she said; "and if nobody will help me, he'll die!"
>
> "Walk out of the room," cried the master, "and let me never hear a word more about him! None here care what becomes of him; if you do, act the nurse; if you do not, lock him up and leave him." '

There is no mistake here about the response we must make: Heathcliff's brutal callousness is as unpardonable as possible since the dying lad is his own son. But immediately on this follows Zillah's own reaction to an identical plea for help from Cathy:

> 'Then she began to bother me, and I said I'd had enough plague with the tiresome thing; we each had our tasks, and hers was to wait on Linton, Mr Heathcliff bid me leave that labour to her.'

This is only a softened version of Heathcliff's reply. But Zillah is no monster and she has an uneasy sense that she must justify herself to Nelly, as is evident in the worried but self-protective narrative that follows:

> 'How they managed together I can't tell. I fancy he fretted a great deal, and moaned hisseln, night and day; and she had precious little rest, one could guess by her white face, and heavy eyes—she sometimes came into the kitchen all wildered like, and looked as if she would fain beg assistance; but I was not going to disobey the master: I never dare disobey him, Mrs Dean, and though I thought it wrong that Kenneth [the doctor] should not be sent for, it was no concern of mine, either to advise or complain; and I always refused to meddle. Once or twice, after we had gone to bed, I've happened to open my door again, and seen her sitting crying, on the stairs' top; and then I've shut myself in quick, for fear of being moved to interfere. I did pity her then, I'm sure: still I didn't want to lose my place, you know!'

This, while pointing out of the book at the reader, more immediately acts as a check on an easily righteous condemnation of Heathcliff, who is now seen as being not so much worse than the self-respecting, chapel-going Zillah (her godly upbringing indicated by the Biblical name chosen by pious parents); Heathcliff differs only in being brutally honest instead of, like Zillah, complaisant in callousness owing to selfishness and ill-will. The corollary, that we must recognize in Zillah's self-adjust-ments a likeness to everyone's excuses for failing to behave in accordance with standards we are uneasily aware we subscribe to, is subsiduary though inescapable. And if we think about it we realise that this technique has been used from the start of the novel. At the opening, setting the pattern, Mr Lockwood's horror (ours too) at the brutal attitudes prevailing at the farmhouse—the point of opening the novel with his report of his two visits there—at their shocking refusal to adopt the ordinary code of civility and even a minimal consideration for a visitor, is underlined by Lockwood's dismay at finding that what he had first put down to a refined misanthropy in Heathcliff, such as he affects himself, is a genuine savagery and malevolence, so that he feels he has strayed into a nightmare world. And Lockwood's horror of the household at Wuthering Heights is immediately offset by *our* horror at *him* when he then, in a real nightmare, brutally fights off the child begging (as he had just done himself) to be let in after losing the way on the moor:

'. . . my fingers closed on the fingers of a little, ice-cold hand! The intense horror of nightmare came over me: I tried to draw back my arm, but the hand clung to it, and a most melancholy voice sobbed, "Let me in—let me in" "Who are you?" I asked, struggling, meanwhile, to disengage myself. "Catherine Linton", it replied shiveringly. "I'm come home: I'd lost my way on the moor!" As it spoke I discerned, obscurely, a child's face looking through the window. Terror made me cruel; and finding it useless to attempt shaking the creature off, I pulled its wrist on to the broken pane, and rubbed it to and fro till the blood ran down and soaked the bedclothes: still it wailed, "Let me in" and maintained its tenacious gripe, almost maddening me with fear. . . . I hurriedly piled the books up in a pyramid against it, and stopped my ears to exclude the lamentable prayer. .... "Begone!" I shouted, "I'll never let you in, not if you beg for twenty years." '

Of course we don't suppose that his waking self would have gone to such lengths (he knows it was cruel) but, we must feel, his savage response in the dream to the ghost-child's plea for compassion is instinctive; so that under the civilized surface there is a Wuthering Heights self buried, and not made more attractive by his explanation 'Terror made me cruel'. This alerts us, right at the beginning, to a general theme in the novel, that concealing or denying the realities of human nature, shrinking from facing the facts, is to court disaster—the gently-bred Linton children show up badly at Wuthering Heights, with their own mean and cowardly brand of ill-feelings; only when Isabella is plunged into the realities of life at the farm does she become capable of courage, aware of her true self and her eyes opened to Heathcliff's, and able to take the initiative. Thus Catherine's famous speech to Nelly beginning 'I *am* Heathcliff' has no need of a mystical interpretation in so far as meaning can be extracted from it; Catherine is testifying that the qualities Heathcliff has and which Edgar's code has tried to suppress (because though they are necessary to maintain life at Wuthering Heights they seem shocking at the Grange) —that these qualities are essential parts of herself now, and that trying to outlaw them and tame herself will prove disastrous. The idyll of her early married life could never have lasted, for her suppressed irritation with and contempt for Edgar is there to be touched off by Heathcliff's reappearance. He releases the now repressed part of her nature (the 'half savage'), which has no relation to the fact that she is happy with Edgar as a lover—we had heard in Chapter IX that she had accepted Edgar on

the assumption that she would never have to be separated
from Heathcliff so that she would be able both to have
her cake and eat it—a childish fallacy. [Nelly had told
her that would not do and tried to show her the dangers
of marrying Edgar in such circumstances.] It is Edgar's
genuine inability to understand why she rejoices in
Heathcliff's return that shocks Catherine into awareness of a gulf between her husband and herself and
which undercuts their happily consummated physical
love. Edgar in fact is guilty in failing her at this crisis—
like Jules he is imaginatively inadequate as well as
too civilized to master his wife by the only means
she could understand, a display of moral and physical
strength. Tenderness, and any fine appeal to the civilized
code, are despised or resented by her as by Roché's
Kate.

In each novel the wife therefore never becomes inte-
grated or truly mature. Both Roché's Kate and Emily
Brontë's Catherine behave like spoiled children who vent
their dissatisfactions by destroying the men they need to
dominate. Emily Brontë's genius has shown Catherine to
be literally a spoiled child (the 'marred child' of Nelly's
observation) by giving us her early history; and Catherine
Linton who is nevertheless only a lost child trying to find
her way home is the ghost who is our first knowledge of
her, just as in her transported state in Chapter XII she
recognizes what has brought her to her deathbed. When
her self-torments begin to tell on her, then she reveals the
child's egocentric delusion: ' "Oh, I've been haunted,
Nelly! I begin to fancy you don't like me. How strange!
I thought, though everybody hated and despised each
other, they could not avoid loving me. And they have all
turned to enemies in a few hours." '

I've been trying to show that the complexity, subtlety and richness of texture of *Wuthering Heights* point to a far greater achievement in insight and wisdom than a comparable novel of apparently greater sophistication and emancipation where sexual relations are concerned, and that *Jules et Jim* though in part treating the same theme, and with the advantage of first-hand experience, is actually less instructive about the human problems both novels are concerned with. It is true that Roché offers no more than a record of two men's experience of Woman, a record that, while avoiding any moral conclusion, indeed suggesting that any is impossible, sets up a moral vacuum in which the characters merely exhibit themselves, so that the characteristic reaction of reviewers was to admire and endorse the heroine. While Roché seems to share the view that his Kate is a splendid creature, there is no doubt that Emily Brontë's attitude to Catherine is not indulgent. She provides no generalisations either about Woman or Life; the impression her novel leaves, of responsibility and impersonality, is endorsed by an insufficiently known report on her by Charlotte's lifelong friend Ellen Nussey who had known the Brontë family since they were school-girls together: 'Emily's extreme reserve seemed impenetrable, yet she was intensely lovable; she invited confidence in her moral power'. Her sister Charlotte stresses Emily's intellectual superiority: 'In some points I consider Emily somewhat of a theorist: now and then she broaches ideas which strike my sense as much more daring and original than practical; her reason may be in advance of mine, but certainly it often travels a different road', and she felt the presence of something disquieting of which she was clearly in awe: 'The tie of sister is near and dear indeed, and I think a certain harshness in her powerful and peculiar character only makes me cling to her more' (when Emily was dying).

Wuthering Heights is highly (though never obtrusively) schematic and the demonstration of the corrective case-history of the second part is not just a matter of winding up the story and restoring the land to the legitimate heirs. If it had stopped with the death of Catherine and the virtual withdrawal from life of Heathcliff and Edgar (the point at which *Jules et Jim* ends) it would have been unsatisfactory. *Jules et Jim*, we can see in comparison, doesn't tell us enough about women to show that Kate does not represent a general truth, as its author seems to imply, or one to which there is no alternative. The second half of Emily Brontë's novel however contains much that is indispensable to the true reading of the first half. The young Cathy's first visit to the farmhouse where her innocent ideas about her status are seen to be ridiculous, as well as offensive to the workers there who serve only their chosen master and are not servile, is characteristically conveyed through spirited dialogue: ' "What's the matter? Get my horse, I say." "I'll see thee damned before I be *thy* servant!" growled the lad (Hareton) . . . "How dare he speak so to me? Mustn't he be made to do as I ask him? You bring the pony," she exclaimed, turning to the woman. "Softly, Miss, you'll lose nothing by being civil. . . . I was never hired to serve you." ' Cathy has had that Linton education which is seen to be finally purged when, having recognized Hareton's merits and her own needs, she freely chooses him as her husband, to become Catherine Earnshaw like her mother; but she has moved in the opposite direction from her mother who, born Catherine Earnshaw, became Catherine Linton of Thrushcross Grange—even though, with the progress of social history, they have to abandon Wuthering Heights to be farmed by old Joseph and settle at the Grange as gentry. Cathy's mother had abandoned the degraded Heathcliff but her daughter generously takes the lad he has formed on that very pattern for revenge, thus righting the wrong. Another stage in her development is seen in Chapter XXIV where accepting Linton Heathcliff's apologia (that he cannot help being what he is) she says: 'I felt I must forgive him'. But the forgiveness carries with it the recognition that she is committed to him and has 'learnt to endure his selfishness and spite with nearly as little resentment as his sufferings'. The hard road begun when she refused to enter into competition with Linton in unkindness is completed when she has tended him till his death, and gone through the pangs of rebirth. Our attention is focussed on this in one of the most memorable passages in the book. Cathy has roused the unwilling Zillah to bid her tell Heathcliff his son is dying at last.

> I delivered Catherine's message. He cursed to himself, and in a few minutes came out with a lighted candle, and proceeded to their room. I followed. Mrs Heathcliff was seated by the bedside, with her hands folded on her knees. Her father-in-law went up, held the light to Linton's face, looked at him, and touched him; afterwards he turned to her.
> ' "Now—Catherine", he said, "how do you feel?"
> 'She was dumb.
> ' "How do you feel, Catherine?" he repeated.
> ' "He's safe, and I'm free," she answered: "I should feel well—but," she continued with a bitterness she couldn't conceal, 'you have left me so long to struggle against death, alone, that I feel and see only death! I feel like death!"
> 'And she looked like it, too.' Zillah reports.

Cathy has still a long spell to serve before she is really

free, however. The admirable resistance the thoroughly masculine Hareton puts up to her inherited impulses (she also is a Catherine) to torment and manipulate him as soon as she sees he loves her, helps her on the way to maturity. The last sign of the old Eve in her is the attempt to provoke a battle between Hareton and Heathcliff— ' "If you strike me, Hareton will strike you" she said'— (just as her mother had deliberately provoked the fight between Heathcliff and Edgar). Her first instinct after securing Hareton's friendship and affection is to prove and show her power by making a violent scene to break the attachment between Hareton and Heathcliff (which exists in spite of all that has gone before, is completely convincing, and not the least of the proofs of Emily Brontë's genius). But on finding that Hareton has loyal feelings towards Heathcliff that are filial and make a tie beyond reasoning with, 'which it would be cruel to attempt to loosen', Nelly notes that 'She showed a good heart thenceforth, in avoiding both complaints and expressions of antipathy concerning Heathcliff; and confessed to me her sorrow that she had endeavoured to raise a bad spirit between him and Hareton.' She shows herself, unlike her mother, capable of self-education and not least in such remarkable restraint where her enemy was concerned; even more perhaps in tolerating a relation between men that excludes herself, but which, it seems to be implied, is essential to their being men (Roché and D. H. Lawrence both make this point more clearly). Cathy brings gaiety into Hareton's life, 'sticking primroses into his plate of porridge' and planning a garden with him by importing plants from the Grange, effective symbolic gestures, like the present of books she has made Hareton to express her repentance and change of heart towards him. She even accepts the necessity for replanting the fruit-bushes and relegating her flower-garden to an unwanted corner (Chapter XXXIV).

Cathy's selfless devotion to her tormenting husband Linton reminds us of Edgar's tenderness to his broken wife in *her* decline: this combination of inheritances from both sides in Cathy is clearly offered as something ponderable about the nature of the human family in general and an assertion of the novelist's belief in free-will as well as in psychological and sociological determinism.[1] The chosen ground is intended to be representative. ' "Oh, here we are the same as anywhere else, when you get to know us" ' says Nelly to Lockwood, rebutting his idea that 'in these regions' people are different from elsewhere. This theme gets other illustrations, notably, and very appropriately since his ideas on the subject are theological, from old Joseph. We recall his sardonic delight on witnessing Linton Heathcliff's murderous outburst against his cousin Hareton: ' "Thear that's t'father!" he cried. "That's father! We've allus summut uh orther side in us." ' Joseph had earlier identified the mother in Linton when the boy refused to eat the family meal of porridge. Nelly noted the 'perverse will' Cathy showed in childhood, like her mother's. And so on.

And these elements which give depth to the novel are enclosed in a sociological whole which serves as the framework of a parable or moral fable of extended interest. Think of what the household at the Heights comprised, with old Joseph, who refuses his portion of Christmas

---

[1] In this, as in the combination of convincing realism and symbolic action in which the belief finds expression, *Wuthering Heights* is remarkably similar to *Great Expectations*. The latter too is a work of art which also contains a sociological novel on the surface.

fare on principle and deplores even the hymns Nelly sings because they sound like 'songs', raising the voice of the traditional Puritanism (though wise as well as harsh); while Nelly offsets him with her equally traditional pagan enjoyment of life, of folk-song and ballad as well as of rearing babies and sympathising with love-affairs. ' "This is 'Faery Annie's Wedding'—a bonny tune—it goes to a dance" ' is Nelly's mischievous reply to Joseph's groans that ' "Aw cannut oppen t'Blessed Book, bud yah set up them glories tuh Sattan." ' Yet they are equally indispensable, Joseph as devoted farmer and Nelly as nurse and housemother. And in another respect Joseph is indispensable too: one of his functions is to offer his own, a rigid religious, interpretation of all events as they happen, so that he sees Heathcliff's life, for example, as a drama of the wicked man whose soul the Devil in due course inevitably collects—for which judgment he falls on his knees beside the corpse to thank God. This is not of course the novelist's view, but it registers her understanding of an important moral vein in the English tradition, one which has fed both folk and 'literary' literature. The novelist is careful to show that Isabella's and the two Catherines' contemptuous attitudes to Joseph are not justified, though their dislike of him is understandable. His piety, for instance, is not hypocrisy as they assume, but a true natural piety expressed in the only idiom he commands other than his everyday dialect—it is the traditional language of Puritanism, of course, as when he calls food 't'precious gifts uh God'—and his sour disapproval of both Isabella and Cathy on the grounds that they are idle inmates where everyone else works, is as reasonable and sound as his anger at Catherine's effect on young Heathcliff which has caused the lad to carelessly

leave the gate open so that the pony gets into the cornfield.
His duty to the farm, to his master, and to God's laws, are
not separate duties in his mind but form together a rule
of life. In fact, a Shakespearean character.[1] The whole
social pattern provided for us by the farm-house at the
Heights, with its house-place shared by master and man,
is created for us as something to be respected, and regretted when it is superseded, whatever its limitations.
There all were united in their efforts to make farming
possible—the heroic human enterprise of struggling with
nature for a living and being formed by that struggle, in
this hard country where, as Lockwood notes for us in the
very opening, the north wind slants the stunted firs and
'the gaunt thorns all stretch their limbs one way as if
craving alms of the sun', a struggle which does not permit
mellow memories such as give charm to *Adam Bede* and
Silas Marner. The ethos of the household evokes the
England of Squire Western (who would have been quite
at home there—a fact that suggests that a historical
eighteenth-century rural society is the author's aim) at a
time when this was being superseded by the new gentility
of Thrushcross Grange—where servants live in their own
quarters and know their place (unlike old Joseph whose
scolding voice can never be avoided) and where the
children are kept from the realities of life in an Early

[1] It is characteristic of *Wuthering Heights* that though Emily Brontë sees
how old Joseph affects her Catherines and Isabellas, she makes it clear that
she is perfectly aware that there are other points of view from which he
makes a better showing—he has dignity, utility and even higher virtues,
and an unprejudiced examination of all he says and does himself (ignoring
what others say of him) proves this. But concentration on the 'metaphysical'
account of *Wuthering Heights* has lost sight of the realistic novel it really
is. And when I say 'Shakespearean' I mean also that Joseph is an indication
of his creator's indebtedness to Shakespeare for novelistic method and
technique that she could have learnt nowhere else.

Victorian world (it seems, though prophetically) of papas and mammas, parlours and picture-books. We remember that Nelly and others have said that it is healthier at the Heights than at the Grange.

The plight of Catherine Earnshaw is thus presented as at once a unique personal history, a method of discussing what being a woman means, and a tragedy of being caught between socially incompatible cultures, for each of which there is much to be said for and against. Perhaps what *Jules et Jim* chiefly shows, without intending to, is the worse danger of existence in a world that gives no guidance, imposes no restraints and in which conscience and obligations are unknown. That Emily Brontë intended to create a coherent, deeply responsible novel whose wisdom should be recognized as useful we can have no doubt, and this is supported by what Mrs Gaskell reported Charlotte as telling her that her sister suffered from the uncomprehending reception of her novel:

> But Emily—poor Emily—the pangs of disappointment as review after review came out about *Wuthering Heights* were terrible. Miss Brontë said she had no recollections of pleasure or gladness about *Jane Eyre*, every such feeling was lost in seeing Emily's resolute endurance yet knowing what she felt.

When Charlotte and Emily were at the school in Brussels, in 1842, M. Héger proposed to teach the sisters to improve their French by setting them to imitate the style of some of the best French authors. While Charlotte acquiesced Emily refused, saying 'she saw no good to be derived from it; and that, by adopting it, they should lose all originality of thought and expression'. 'Originality of thought and expression': yes, one sees that this was prized by the author of *Wuthering Heights* and that it made some sacrifices seem negligible to her—sacrifices of plausibility, of consecutiveness, of proportion, even of consistency,—which could often have been saved if the novelist had cared about such things. Besides the unexplained hiatus in Heathcliff's life and his disparate selves, the most careless gesture is the history of the little savage Hareton, whom we have glimpsed in childhood stoning and cursing visitors and 'hanging a litter of puppies from a chairback', Heathcliff's promising pupil; the unlikelihood of *this* Hareton's turning up as a generous-minded and warm-hearted youth not unfit to marry Cathy, seems clear. But we need hardly notice the anomaly for Hareton is seen fragmentarily and not in chronological order at that, he is only there to serve different purposes and doesn't matter in himself till the final drama with Cathy. We notice also that the novelist has attempted to correct the disparity between the child and the youth Hareton by bridge episodes reported by Zillah, where Hareton shows to advantage compared with Linton (' "and if Hareton, for pity, comes to amuse him—Hareton is not bad-natured, though he's rough—they're sure to part, one swearing and the other crying" ') and in Chapter XXX where he is seen to have tried to get Heathcliff to let him sit up with the dying Linton to relieve Cathy. In fact, throughout *Wuthering Heights*, we may see, unless we refuse to do so, that a true novelist is at work, whose material was real life and whose concern was to promote a fine awareness of the nature of human relations and the problem of maturity.

And we may reflect on the care taken with an even less important character (apparently)—Frances Earnshaw, the 'rush of a lass' whom Hindley brings home after his father's death. We see her first through Catherine's girlish diary, read by the uncomprehending Lockwood, where Frances figures as ridiculous because unashamedly in love with her husband, and disagreeable because disapproving of the 'gypsy' Heathcliff as a playmate for her young sister-in-law Catherine. Then follows Nelly's account of her coming to the Heights as a bride, the kind of 'foreigner' whom the natives 'don't take to', in spite of her delight at 'the white floor and huge glowing fire-place, at the pewter dishes and delf-case, and dog-kennel and the wide space there was to move about in where they usually sat'—at, that is, the 'house-place', often called simply and significantly 'the house', which was used as a common living-room by the domestic- and farm-workers as well as by the family, and even by the dogs (essential members of a farming household and for whom built-in provision was made, as Lockwood noted, in 'an arch under the dresser'). But the result of her coming is that Joseph and Nelly are turned out into the back-kitchen. Frances's appreciation, that of a 'foreigner', was of the picturesque appearance only. She could not comprehend the reality of the purpose served by 'the house', so essential to the proper functioning of the small farm, and this underlines her unsuitability as wife to the master. Her folly is shown in another way, by her helping to orient her young sister-in-law towards the Lintons' idea of gentility and encouraging Catherine's vanity and egotism. Frances thus belongs to the sociological meaning of the novel. But, as with everyone else in the novel, she is also something more. The final impression we are (deliberately) left with is not that of a silly woman; we can't write her off and she is not predictable. Her courage and spirit in refusing to admit that she is suffering and doomed, her raptures at the birth of her boy, her 'gay heart that never failed her' as Nelly reports with a mixture of admiration and compassion that we must share and that culminates in the touching account of her actual dying, as well as the fact that her loss leaves her husband so desolate that he begins to drink himself to death—prove that the novelist has something more profoundly human to convey through Frances. For one thing, before we are shown what Catherine makes of marriage we are given a norm to compare that with. And then there is the moving history itself of a domestic tragedy. Frances has no 'metaphysical' meaning and is not indispensable to the plot, but she makes an important contribution to the truly human novel which *Wuthering Heights* is. How can we not feel that Frances's poignant death, the husband's life left empty and the fatal loss to her child of a mother, did not spring from the novelist's need to register the memories of the comparable Brontë tragedy? Like Hindley, Patrick Brontë had been reared on a small farm, managed to get to the university, and brought a delicate bride (from warm Cornwall) to a bleak northern home where, after great suffering cheerfully borne, she died prematurely, leaving six little children (when Emily was two), a disaster for the family that affected their whole lives. As for the horrors of a home containing a desperate drunkard, she had no need to draw them from anywhere but their own household: even the gentle Anne Brontë felt obliged to make a novel to record that.

I would make a plea, then, for criticism of *Wuthering Heights* to turn its attention to the human core of the novel, to recognize its truly human centrality. How can we fail to see that the novel is based on an interest in, concern for, and knowledge of, real life? We cannot do it justice, establish what the experience of reading it really is, by making analyses of its lock and window imagery, or by explaining it as being concerned with children of calm and children of storm, or by putting forward such bright ideas as that '*Wuthering Heights* might be viewed at long range as a variant of the demon-lover motif' (*The Gates of Horn*, H. Levin) or that 'Nelly Dean is Evil'—these are the products of an age which conceives literary criticism as either a game or an industry, not as a humane study. To learn anything of this novel's true nature we must put it into the category of novels it belongs to—I have specified *Women in Love* and *Jules et Jim* and might add *Anna Karenina* and *Great Expectations*—and recognize its relation to the social and literary history of its own time. The human truths *Wuthering Heights* is intended to establish are, it is necessary to admit, obscured in places and to varying degrees by discordant trimmings or left-overs from earlier writings or stages of its conception; for these, stylistic and other evidence exists in the text. Nor could we expect such complexity and such technical skill to have been achieved in a first novel otherwise; it is necessary to distinguish what is genuine complexity from what is merely confusion. That there is the complexity of accomplished art we must feel in the ending, ambiguous, impersonal, disquieting but final. And when we compare the genius devoted to creating Nelly Dean, Joseph, Zillah, Frances, Lockwood, the two Catherines, and to setting them in significant action, with the very perfunctory attention given to Heathcliff and Hareton as wholes (attention directed only when these two are wheeled out to perform necessary parts at certain points in the exposition of the theme to which—like Isabella and Edgar Linton—they are subsidiary) then we can surely not misinterpret the intention and the nature of the achievement of *Wuthering Heights*.

THE NORTHERN FARMER, OLD STYLE

To give some grounding to what the novelist was trying to convey to us as the traditional culture of the Yorkshire moorlands and its characteristic human product, contrasting so radically with the conventional norm of the English gentry (represented by the Lintons of Thrushcross Grange), I have selected the following as coming closest to the description of the farm-house at the Heights. I found it in the Introduction to a collection, published in 1881, of anecdotes and tales serially published 1853–1857, J. H. Dixon's *Chronicles and Stories of the Craven Dales*. This introduction, by the Rev. Robert Collyer, a native of those parts, recalls his boyhood there in the eighteen-thirties—this takes us back to Emily Brontë's girlhood, as she was born in 1818. It is the more interesting for not being written with *Wuthering Heights* at all in mind, and for being by a minister. The Craven Dales, though also in the West Riding of Yorkshire, are in a different part of it from the Brontës' Haworth; this bears out the representativeness of the home, people and life at the Heights as witness to an originally pagan, Scandinavian farming culture, once common to much of northern England, with all its rugged qualities that made for survival, and in particular its great antiquity and its almost unchanged character in Emily Brontë's youth. Even the 'wuthering' wind features in Collyer's reminiscences as formative; we note too the panelled bed which has a memorable part in the novel, and we get a juster idea of what Nelly meant (in Chapter XVII) by saying that she 'insisted on the funeral [of Hindley Earnshaw] being respectable'.

'I find myself wishing also that Dr Dixon had written one more chapter for us—a chapter containing a picture of a genuine old Craven homestead and its inmates, because no man could have done it so well. I have such a picture in my mind. It is almost half a century old. It is a picture of a sturdy, low thatched house, in which the first thing that attracted my child's eyes was a wonderful bedstead of black oak, built up all round with oaken boards for curtains, panelled and carven, with a door through which you went to find the piled-up feathers, shutting and bolting it after you, so that, if the burglars came, you could get ready for a fight. Then there was a settle of black oak, with a very old date on it, and a chair to match, of a discomfort equal to Calvin's chair in Geneva. A quaint old clock in the corner, with a face of brass on which there was a picture of the sun of such a rotund jollity that it has touched the original with lines of laughter to my mind through all the years. The great "fleak" for the oatbread comes out next, and the flitches of beef and bacon hanging from the black beams. Then the flagged floor with fine sand for a carpet, and the great peat fire with its aromatic pungency; the rack against the wall with its splendid store of pewter plates, the great oaken dresser under it, and a carven "kist" where it was whispered the old man kept his "brass". He was a man of the real old Craven breed. I used to think he could not speak in level tones, but must needs address you as if you stood at some distance, a habit caught, I suppose, from talking in the teeth of the wind which blows for ever across the Craven uplands. His dress was but slightly altered from that of the peasants in Chaucer's time. He cut his grass with a scythe, and his grain with a sickle, and hated the French, though he could not tell you why. It was the smouldering hate, no doubt, of 800 years, kept alive ever since the Conqueror laid Craven waste. . . . His good wife saved a bit of the old yule-log, wrapped in white linen, to kindle the new withal, and would let no fire go out of the house during the days between "owd and new Kersmas". The old man believed fervently in witches and t'gy-trash.[1] He

[1] The guytrash was a supernatural northern animal generally taking the form of a large shaggy dog with saucer-eyes which was to be met on field-paths and in churchyards after dusk, appearing to warn of sudden death in the family—if it looked you in the face you were the one doomed; 'trash' being a verb signifying to walk wearily through mire. It may be remembered that Jane Eyre, meeting Mr Rochester's dog Pilot in such circumstances, took it for 'the Gytrash'; Charlotte used what Mrs Gaskell describes as 'the grim superstitions of the North', 'implanted in her by the servants who believed in them' with very good effect in *Jane Eyre*, and so did Emily, as can be seen throughout *Wuthering Heights*, particularly in Chapter XII (*v.* Appendix C).

was, in truth, as I think of him now and remember his queer ways, one third pagan, one third catholic, and the rest was little better than veneer—I imagine, dating from the Reformation. So he lived as his fathers had lived time out of all mind. They were there on the moor side—the warm side dipping well toward the meadows and woods—in Earl Edwin's time; saw the Percies and Romillies and Cliffords come and go, while they still held on eating their brown- and oaten-bread and bacon, and drinking their milk and "honey-drink" and beer. They will last to the crack of doom. When the old man's time came to die, it comes back to me how "he gave commandment concerning his bones" and would have everything done "i t'owd way". I think, indeed, he had a dim idea that he would be there as a sort of silent spectator, and might be troubled if things went wrong. So he would have no wine and biscuit served at the funeral—"nēa nut he". They must brew plenty o' drink and bake plenty o' spice cēak and cut it thick, and hand it round at least three times, and everybody must eat and drink their fill. How one hungry growing lad did enjoy that funeral, to be sure; but he wist not, any more than the old man in his coffin, that it was the last long-lingering echo and refrain of the funeral feasts of his pagan ancestors a thousand years ago. And I can remember how they decked his shroud very much as if Ophelia had been there to direct them. There were violets and pansies, columbines and daisies, sweet thyme, rosemary, and rue, for that was the ancient way; and he must be laid away as he had lived, with all the old rites and observances about his dust. Then as they bore him to his burial along the green shadowy lanes to Bolton they sang old funeral chants Job might have written, and Jeremiah set to music, they were so shorn of all that sheds a new radiance on death and the grave.'

'VIOLENCE'

Though we are now less inclined than earlier critics to think violence of feeling and action so improbable as to imply something abnormal in a novelist who depicts it, yet criticism still boggles, it seems, at the violence in *Wuthering Heights*. This, about which so much has been written, certainly needs distinguishing as to kinds. In general, the intention at the outset to create a tragedy on a Shakespearian pattern, specifically, as I've suggested, by drawing on the sub-plot of *Lear* (there are also references to *Lear* in the text), has brought with it a sense of being in the *Lear* universe, though it is Heathcliff who (understandably, if my account of his conception is admitted) seems to belong there most consistently— that is, who, for the novelist, is a reminder to put in such features whenever he is operative. Sometimes the horrors of the *Lear* world are almost dutifully inserted, as the knife under Isabella's ear, the fight between Heathcliff and Hindley and the account of Hindley's death—all in Chapter XVII; though none of these seems to me to achieve the horror of the plucking out of Gloucester's eyes, which no doubt inspired them. The worst and almost the only genuine wounds received in *Wuthering Heights* are given by the tongue, as we can prove by reading the extremely painful scene of violence between Catherine, Heathcliff and Edgar in Chapter XI where the only physical violence is the blow Edgar is forced to give Heathcliff and which does no more than 'take his breath for a moment'. Much of the violence is the result of women's characteristic provocation to which the men can react only by blows—this is equally true of *Jules et Jim* where there is also a good deal of violence—by blows or, as in the final parting between Heathcliff and the dying Catherine, when he is goaded by her 'wild vindictiveness' and her tearing out his hair, into bruising her by holding fast her arms. The most horrible cruelty, like Lockwood's rubbing the child-ghost's wrist against the broken window to free himself from its grasp, is a nightmare only, and is kept as such before us (as unreal) by his having first broken the window by thrusting his own arm through without suffering; while other happenings of gratuitous cruelty such as Heathcliff's hanging the pet dog Fanny, and Heathcliff's allegedly setting a trap over the lapwings' nest which starved the nestlings, are symbolic (Fanny represents her mistress Isabella who is eloping with Heathcliff to her doom, and the dog's life is actually saved by Nelly; while we have only the delirious Catherine's word for the lapwing exploit in a speech in the tradition of Ophelia's and Lucy Ashton's mad utterances). Another class of horrors are juvenile and seem to be left over from the Gondal game (which Emily and Anne were still playing together as late as June 30, 1845—*Wuthering Heights* being written, it seems, in its present form in the autumn and winter 1845-1846): for instance, Isabella's account of Heathcliff's looking in at the window when 'his black countenance looked blightingly through . . . his sharp cannibal teeth gleamed through the dark' etc.—such horrendous passages contrast with the perfectly simple, sincere and delicately poetic or forcefully colloquial language of the maturer parts. Little Hareton's hanging a whole litter of puppies from the chair-back as Isabella departs (it is quite out of character with everything subsequent in his history) seems to be thrown in as a last proof that she has supped full of horrors and is, as she says, 'escaped from purgatory'.

Besides the need to emulate what seemed essential to an Elizabethan tragedy, Emily Brontë, I have no doubt, was also deliberately trying to realise a historical past (the novel takes place in the eighteenth century) when manners were generally supposed to have been brutal and, in out-of-the-way places, lawless. We may note here the indication provided as to lawlessness by Heathcliff's having been able to bribe Linton's lawyer from making a new will before Edgar's death which would have kept the daughter's property out of Heathcliff's hands. Certainly there is an impression of effort to achieve the effect of a past age but one historically accurate.[1]

[1] She would have got the tone of the period from their old servant, nurse and faithful friend Tabby who died in their service at above eighty and whom I deduce was born in 1769—in the same decade, that is, as Catherine Earnshaw is supposed to have been born; Tabby of course would have inherited and passed on the traditions of the generation before

Charlotte seems to endorse this when, in her preface to the 1850 edition of the novel, she describes the 'harshly manifested passions' of the 'rugged moorland squires' of local history as authentic models for the book, telling how her sister steeped herself in 'those tragic and terrible traits of which, in listening to the secret annals of every rude vicinage, the memory is sometimes compelled to receive the impress' as the reason for the 'sombre' materials of the novel. I don't know why subsequent critics should be convinced they can write this off, discrediting both Charlotte and Mrs Gaskell as evidence in this respect; Mrs Gaskell gathered supporting data from many oral sources. Mrs Gaskell wrote from Haworth during her first visit to Charlotte: 'They are a queer people up there. Small landed proprietors—dwelling on one spot since Q. Elizabeth —& lately adding marvellously to their incomes by using the water power of the becks in the woollen manufacture which had sprung up during the last 50 years:—uneducated—unrestrained by public opinion—for their equals in position are as bad as themselves and the poor, besides being densely ignorant, are all dependent on their employers.'

So all things considered, it does seem preposterous to feed such utterly disparate features of *Wuthering Heights* as can be thrust into the one category of 'Violence' into an academic computer in order to produce a cover-all interpretative thesis which confidently classifies the novelist as a case.

her own birth also, the period of Fielding's and Smollett's novels with their evidence of an age in which a good deal of violence, brutality and domestic harshness was manifest.

SUPERSTITIONS AND FOLKLORE

The first half of Chapter XII, in which Catherine explains herself, partly in delirium and partly conscious, and which is crucial to her history, depends in places on the reader's understanding Yorkshire superstitions and folk-lore. But there is nothing esoteric about them, they were once general in northern England and also in various other parts of the country.

Ripping open the pillow in her fever Catherine says:

'Ah, they put pigeons' feathers in the pillows—no wonder I couldn't die. Let me take care to throw it on the floor when I lie down.' This is because it was widely believed that dying persons could not be released from their sufferings and die a peaceful death if there were any game-birds' feathers, particularly pigeons', in either the pillow or feather-mattress on which they lay,[1] so it was important to see that only domestic poultry feathers went into the home-made bedding. There were therefore unlikely to be either wild duck's or pigeons' or moor-cock's or lapwing's feathers in Catherine's pillow at Thrushcross Grange, as she alleges, and the soliloquy is to be understood as an expression of her longing to be released from the Grange and to fly free across the moor, and her sense of being prevented; she identifies herself with the lapwing: 'Bonny bird; wheeling over our heads in the middle of the moor. It wanted to get to its nest, for the clouds had touched the swells, and it felt rain coming.' Then follows the obscure but unforgettable image of the lapwings' nest that Heathcliff set a trap over for

---

[1] Cf. Mrs Gaskell's novel *Mary Barton* (1848) where the characters though also northern are Lancashire folk: ' "Did he die easy?" "He was restless all night long." "And in course thou plucked the pillow away? Thou didst not! Well! with thy bringing up and thy learning, thou mightst have known that were the only help in such a case. There were pigeons' feathers in the pillow, depend on't. To think of two grown-up folk like you and Mary, not knowing death could never come easy to a person lying on a pillow with pigeons' feathers in!" ' (Chap. XXXVI).

the old birds, so starving the nestlings, which she and Heathcliff saw in the winter as skeletons trapped in the nest. While the general intention of the distressing simile is clear, it seems to me unwise to try and nail it down by an interpretation. It is the point where she approaches Shakespeare most nearly in a chapter that is as Shakespearean in dramatic and poetic effect as a novel in prose can be, one feels.

Nelly takes the pillow away from her and her attention is next caught by the mirror; she thinks it the black clothes-press of her childhood bedroom at the Heights and that her face reflected in the mirror is due to candle-light on the piece of furniture. To soothe her, Nelly covers the mirror with a shawl so she will not see her reflection. The sense is not perfectly clear but it seems to me that Nelly's covering it makes her realize that it *was* a mirror, since mirrors were always covered or turned face to the wall immediately after death had taken place in the house, in order that the reflection of the dead spirit might not, as superstition feared, be seen in the glass, with dire consequences to the viewer. Nelly cannot persuade her that it was her own face she saw reflected: ' "Who is it? I hope it will not come out when you are gone! Oh! Nelly, the room is haunted!" ' Then Nelly again reassures her: ' "There's nobody there! It was *yourself*, Mrs Linton." "Myself!" she gasped, "and the clock is striking twelve! It's true, then! That's dreadful!" ' Her fear of a ghost is replaced by a worse fear, that it *was* her own reflection she saw. Sick people, it was held, should not see themselves in a mirror because the soul (thought of as a separate entity like a bird) might easily take flight from the weak body by being projected into the mirror and so bring about the sick person's death. So Catherine, having seen herself in the mirror and hearing the clock strike midnight too, the ghostly hour when spirits walk and death comes, thinks she is about to die. Of course she does want to die and presently dwells on her imminent death as a way of getting out on the moor and recovering Heathcliff, instead of being 'Mrs Linton, the lady of Thrushcross Grange'. The dream in which she thought herself back in the oak-panelled bed, alone for the first time after her father's burial (death is running through her mind continually) was broken, she says, by her waking to find herself stretched on the carpet (where she had fallen in her fit or swoon). But this gave her a dreadful shock—presumably because she thought it meant she was dying since those absolutely on the point of death were removed from the bed and placed on the floor (out of kindness) to die 'naturally'. The premonitions of death in this scene prepare Catherine to accept it with relief so that she thinks she sees a candle in her window on the Heights to guide her home (we now recall Lockwood's dream of the pathetic child-ghost calling itself Catherine Linton trying to get back into its oak-panelled bed), though she knows that 'we must pass Gimmerton Kirk, to go that journey!' Her wrestling to hang out of the window and her commands to Nelly to 'Open the window: throw it wide open!' is not only that she may breathe the air from the hills but would be readily understood as another anticipation of death, since when the moment of death was unmistakably at hand, it was the custom to throw open all doors and windows, that nothing should hinder the flight of the spirit.[1]

Her boast next that as children she and Heathcliff had often stood in the churchyard defying the ghosts of the dead (like Don Giovanni) by inviting them to come, establishes their impious pride which will bring about Heathcliff's death, obsessed by Catherine's ghostly presence—'intolerable torture'—until he can no longer remember to eat or even breathe. She is one ghost that accepts the invitation. Like Don Giovanni he rejects the opportunity to repent Nelly offers him (Chapter XXXIV) and maintains his 'godless indifference' to the last, dying with a sneer on his face, 'girnning at death', as Joseph says of his corpse. In many respects Heathcliff follows the pattern of the original tradition of Don Juan, who, before he became merely a womanizer, was the typical wicked man who broke all the Ten Commandments. There is a suggestion that Heathcliff too has been dragged away

[1] v. E. M. Wright, *Rustic Speech and Folklore* (Oxford, 1914). Mrs Wright (who collaborated with her husband on the English Dialect Dictionary), added that 'In Yorkshire there exists an idea that the door must not be locked for seven years after a death in the house.' All the above death-superstitions can be found documented in her chapter on 'Birth, Marriage and Death Customs' as belonging to Yorkshire (as well as various other parts of England, of course), though some are better explained in Frazer.

to hell (in Joseph's words, 'The divil's harried off his soul'), and at the end of the novel we hear that the country folks believe 'he *walks*', an unquiet spirit. The little boy herding sheep actually sees the ghosts of 'Heathcliff and a woman', and though Nelly dismisses it as imagination fed on gossip (she is not one to see spirits) she also notes that the sheep won't pass the spot. This impartial treatment of belief in the supernatural and of its concomitants, the evocation of a whole pagan mode of thought about life and death, then and there still current, which gave dignity and meaning to a hard and narrow existence, has nothing to do with such romantic or 'Gothic' aberrations as cannibal teeth and the reopening of coffins to look at beloved corpses. It is, rather, a mark of the creative artist's respect for an essential element in the culture she values but sees disappearing, worsted by something less healthy and, in its moral triteness, altogether inferior—Nelly never voices Christian piety or moralisms without their seeming either inadequate or irrelevant. It also implies recognition of the poetry and wisdom inherent in the old beliefs—as in the ballad Nelly sings in her tenderness for her 'little lamb' which was based on a mysterious fact of experience, the profound tie between mother and child.

Another parallel mark of respect for that culture is the novelist's concern to do justice to the local country speech. The dialect, whether in its undiluted form as spoken by old Joseph or in modified forms such as Zillah's, Hareton's and others', is full of life, not only in idiom but in intonation and vocabulary, above all notable for the independent and sensible attitudes it expresses so forcefully. The common people's speech here is so much more lively in general than that of the educated (just as in Scott) that it makes one feel there is some justice in Max Müller's dictum that 'The real and natural life of language is in its dialects.' It is odd that Emily Brontë's ear should be so much better for uneducated than for educated speech, where she is liable to use stilted or literary phrases whenever her imagination had no pressure behind it. It was difficult for her, it seems, to find a staple style (Dickens and other Early Victorian writers betray the same difficulty). This is a specimen of her writing on her twenty-third birthday (three years before writing *Wuthering Heights*): 'It will be a fine warm summer evening, very different from this bleak look-out, and Anne and I will perchance slip out into the garden for a few minutes to peruse our papers.' Literary words like 'peruse' and 'perchance' incongruously mixed with the idiomatic 'slip out' and 'look-out' betray an uncertain taste, and similarly uneasy oscillations can be noticed in the novel—but not often where they matter. This is, however, the literary style used by Catherine in the journal Lockwood reads while trying to get to sleep in the panelled bed at the Heights, a very improbable style for a country child and which, along with some puerilities and long-winded episodes such as the sermon part of Lockwood's nightmare, bear out the supposition that the first three chapters contain some unregenerate writing from an earlier attempt at a novel or this novel.

APPENDIX D

'WUTHERING HEIGHTS' AND 'THE BRIDE OF LAMMERMOOR'

Mrs Gaskell tells us that Sir Walter Scott's writings were among the standard literature owned by Mr Brontë, and in 1834 we find Charlotte writing to a friend who has asked for a reading-list: 'For fiction, read Scott alone; all novels after his are worthless'— proof enough that the Brontë girls read them, and with enthusiasm. My very strong impression is of a considerable carry-over from *The Bride of Lammermoor* to *Wuthering Heights* (and *Lammermoor* and *The Black Dwarf* have enough common elements to coalesce as one united source for inspiration and memory). To start with, *Wuthering Heights* is, in the Scott tradition, a historical and not

a contemporary novel. Then the tone of *Wuthering Heights* is
at times that of Scott, and the doomed Ravenswood is laid under
contribution not only for the pattern of Heathcliff's name but
for his nature and circumstances. Ravenswood early in life gives
himself up to the passion for vengeance on those who have
wronged him; he is characterized by his 'dark and sullen brow'
and, in the words of the heroine's young brother, Henry, 'looked
like a Spanish grandee come to cut our throats and trample our
bodies underfoot', and he does indeed perform acts of desperate
violence. But he is also named *Edgar* in his character of tender
lover to Lucy Ashton, whose family have ruined him and turned
him out of his home and then used him cruelly in respect to Lucy.
He is driven to raging violence when Lucy is induced to give him
up for a more suitable husband, bringing about first her violent
death and then his own. Moreover, violent passions, violent actions
and revenge, omens and dreams, dementia of the heroine, bloody
and supernatural deaths, are common to both novels; Catherine
follows Lucy in being driven out of her senses by the conflicting
claims of lover and bridegroom; Alice the nourice's part is taken
by Nelly Dean and old Caleb's by old Joseph. That Scott founded
his tale and in some detail on the real-life historical case of a Lord
Rutherford and the daughter of the first Lord Stair, must have
given it a desirable authority for a novelist who, as I hold, was not
romancing but concerned to examine the real basis and effects of
love and the relations between the sexes as well as the relations
between child and parent, and who sees all these as inseparable
from their social context in time and place. Here Scott, with his
acute interest in the unique nature of Scottish society and its
historical development was again, as in *The Black Dwarf*, a
highly educational influence and an influence visible directly in
Wuthering Heights. Ravenswood is the last of a noble line, cheated
out of his inheritance and prospects alike by the rising lawyer of
humble Puritan origin who is representative of the new dominant
type and class—inevitably, just as the supersession of the Wuthering
Heights life-form by the world of Thrushcross Grange was
inevitable. No doubt Scott's insights sharpened Emily Brontë's,
but it is proof of her genius that she could recognize such larger
forces operating behind the domestic and personal drama of a

love-story, as her sister Charlotte, for instance, could not.

Scott's serious use of broad Scots in *Lammermoor* must also have decided our novelist to draw on the West Riding dialect for similar effects. An important contribution to the thrilling atmosphere of *Lammermoor* comes from the mouths of village characters who supply the superstitions, second sight, knowledge of the leading characters' histories and dooms; and who provide a chorus-commentary on the progress of the tragedy of the two families involved, as Nelly Dean and old Joseph do. Scott not only suggests dark forces at work through the irrational and traditional beliefs of the countryfolk, but he frequently works through a suggestive symbolism which I imagine is a direct result of his sympathy with the mode of Scottish folksong and ballad, though compared with folk-literature he shows up as clumsy and self-conscious in these efforts. Some comparisons with very similar passages in *Wuthering Heights* will show what a great genius does when it makes them its own. I will cite a diffused and a specific instance.

The chapter that introduces us to Ravenswood ends by suggesting that, like Heathcliff, he was thought to have been under diabolic influence (his death too is uncanny): 'The peasant who shows the ruins of the tower, which still crown the beetling cliff and behold the war of the waves, though no more tenanted save by the seamew and cormorant, even yet affirms, that on this fatal night the Master of Ravenswood, by the bitter exclamations of his despair, evoked some evil fiend, under whose malignant influence the future tissue of incident was woven. Alas! what fiend can suggest more desperate counsels than those adopted under the guidance of our own violent and unresisted passions?' The scene described here, after the tragedy is ended and the participants long dead, provides, with its suggestive imagery of sea eternally at war with cliff and the ruins of the Ravenswood home inhabited now only by symbolic sea-birds, a similar pregnant and melancholy after-picture for the reader to the ending of *Wuthering Heights* (in the last three paragraphs), but how stilted and creaking Scott's prose is and how conventional the moralising! In his Chapter XXIX we have a more instructive parallel. The painful images the delirious Catherine evokes in Chapter XII as a metaphor to express her sense of her position—the images of the lapwing unable to take shelter in its nest and of Heathcliff starving the nestlings to skeletons by setting a trap over the nest for the parent birds—this metaphor and its context has an obvious origin in Scott's set piece when Lucy Ashton, like Catherine in beginning to lose her reason under stress, is roused by Henry's telling her innocently about his falcon which ' "just wets her singles in the blood of the partridge, and then breaks away, and lets her fly; and what good can the poor bird do after that, you know, except to pine and die in the first heather cow or whin-bush she can crawl into?" "Right, Henry— right, very right", said Lucy mournfully, holding the boy fast by the hand; "but there are more riflers in the world than your falcon, and more wounded birds that seek but to die in quiet, that can find neither brake nor whin-bush to hide their heads in." ' Lucy is pathetic, but our sympathy and interest are quite cooled by noting how rationally and logically she makes the case for a parallel between her own situation and the victim's of Henry's anecdote. Emily Brontë is not, like Scott, constrained by rationality, but nevertheless Scott's artificial rhetoric has left its impress in a corresponding vein in some places (the weakest) in her novel, though not here, where what is only skilful rhetoric in Scott has been transformed with Shakespearean power into the rhythmically convincing expression of deep disturbance. But then Catherine Earnshaw is an infinitely more interesting character than Lucy Ashton, and that Emily Brontë should replace Scott's conventional passive heroine by the study of a challenging type of feminine nature is significant of where her interest and talent lay.

We conclude then that Emily Brontë shows herself to have had far greater imaginative power than Scott as well as much greater complexity of feeling and construction, that hers is altogether a finer art than Scott's; but there seems to me no doubt that novels of Scott and tragedies of Shakespeare were equally present in her mind as it organized the insights on which *Wuthering Heights* is based. The sense in which one writer is indebted to others is always interesting, and more particularly in the case of a work which has so generally been claimed to have been as wholly original and unaccountable as *Wuthering Heights*. It may also help us to see exactly in what the true distinction of the work consists.